TOTAL QUALITY
AN EXECUTIVE'S GUIDE
FOR THE 1990s

TOTAL QUALITY
AN EXECUTIVE'S GUIDE
FOR THE 1990s

The Ernst & Young Quality Improvement Consulting Group

AMERICAN SOCIETY OF
QUALITY CONTROL
310 West Wisconsin Avenue
Milwaukee, Wisconsin 53203

BUSINESS ONE IRWIN
Homewood, Illinois 60430

© RICHARD D. IRWIN, INC., 1990

Sponsoring editor: Jim Childs
Project editor: Jean Roberts
Production manager: Carma W. Fazio
Compositor: Carlisle Communications, Ltd.
Typeface: 11/13 Century Schoolbook
Printer: R. R. Donnelley & Sons Company

Library of Congress Cataloging-in-Publication Data

Huge, Ernest C.
    Total quality: an executive's guide for the 1990s / Ernest C. Huge.
        p.   cm.—(The BUSINESS ONE IRWIN APICS series in production management)
    Bibliography: p.
    Includes index.
    ISBN 1-55623-188-1   ISBN 1-55623-364-7
    1. Quality control. 2. Production management—Quality control.
I. Title. II. Series.
TS156.H84   1990
658.5′62—dc20

89–34624
CIP

Printed in the United States of America
7 8 9 0 DO 6 5 4 3 2 1

PREFACE

The world economy has changed forever. After World War II, the world's manufacturing capacity was devastated except in the United States. Given the pent-up demand for goods and having the only significant capability to produce, U.S. companies could sell just about anything they could make. Quantity was much more important than quality. Now, however, the situation is completely reversed; many countries have the capability to compete globally. Because supply now exceeds demand, quality of goods and services dominates. Excess capacity has created intense global competition that, in turn, has spawned a new management paradigm driven by quality. Because it is a new standard for running a business, companies do not have a choice of whether or not to adopt the new philosophy; they only have varying degrees of time, depending upon the competition.

This book describes the new quality paradigm, which goes by many names and encompasses a myriad of acronyms. We have chosen the term *total quality*. The primary purpose of the book is to offer a succinct, but comprehensive, guide for top management, who must lead what amounts to a cultural transformation. Leadership for such a change cannot be delegated. Top managers must lead this change, not only within their own company, but within their industry. Few companies can be world class alone since most depend upon suppliers of goods and services. Their suppliers and their suppliers' suppliers must also become world class.

Such a change requires a very different leader from the traditional U.S. leadership model. The book describes not only what the executive must know, but also what he or she must do to help accomplish this radical change. It is a proactive role for the executive that must not be viewed as a lower-level tactical concern. The key ingredients of a quality improvement strategy include communicating the importance of quality, developing a greater understanding of current and potential customers, taking a companywide approach to quality so that all functions can relate efforts to the ultimate customer, and devising a system to ensure that strategic goals are translated into appropriate actions throughout the company.

The stakes are enormous: U.S. economic well-being and the quality of life that goes with it are on the line. We have seen what has happened to traditionally managed U.S. businesses that have competed with masters of the new paradigm. In the incredibly short time span of 10–20 years, U.S. companies have lost major markets that they previously dominated. As a result of losing the global economic war, the U.S. standard of living has actually eroded. We have been lulled to sleep by some economic savants who reassure us "not to worry, we're transitioning from an industrial to a service society." We have, in fact, transitioned—from the world's leading creditor to the world's leading debtor, from the world's leading exporter of machine tools to the world's leading importer. Our two major export items today are raw materials—scrap metal and paper products. We are in very much the same position as were the original thirteen colonies with respect to Great Britain.

Manufacturing companies were the first to be challenged. Service industries will be next because the new paradigm is universally applicable to all enterprises. Every one of the concepts and principles discussed in this book is equally applicable to service and manufacturing companies. Because of the high stakes, we must shift into high gear very quickly. Our competition is not standing still.

A NOTE ABOUT THIS BOOK

There are no simple answers to the quality puzzle. This book integrates the most important contributions of such renowned quality masters as W. Edwards Deming, Joseph M. Juran, Armand V. Feigenbaum, Genichi Taguchi, Kaoru Ishikawa, Philip B. Crosby, and Shigeo Shingo and combines their insights with the firsthand experience and know-how of the Ernst & Young quality improvement consulting community, some members of which jointly authored this work.

This is not a detailed book about techniques; rather, we hope to give the executive an understanding of the concepts that will be critical to effective competition during the 1990s. We attempt to explain, beginning with top management, what everyone in the organization must do in order to accomplish the overall objective of competitive superiority.

Part 1 explains how to shape a vision of the future and to build commitment to change. It addresses how to lead, plan, and sustain change. To provide an integrated frame of reference for the various topics that make up the new paradigm, Chapter 1 is intended to be an overview of the total book. Part 2 deals with implementing key prerequisites for quality improvement. Part 3 explores several critical aspects concerning the execution of a quality strategy.

While each chapter is written to stand alone, we encourage you to read Part 1 before moving on to other chapters in the book. Hopefully, the succinct format of the book will allow for quick reading.

Ernest C. Huge, Editor

ACKNOWLEDGEMENTS

The authors are indebted to a lot of people for their help, support, and forebearance.

For their endorsement, we thank the Advisory Board of the BUSINESS ONE IRWIN/American Production and Inventory Control Manufacturing Management Series:

Jim Burlingame	Hank Jordan
Eli Goldratt	George Plossl
Elizabeth Haas	Richard Schonberger
Bob Hall	Tom Vollmann
Ed Heard	Clay Whybark

We are especially grateful to Ken Stork of Motorola and Gray Williams of NEC for their extensive insights and suggestions.

In addition to their contributions as authors, Lucy Lytle and Gerald Vasily also provided considerable editorial assistance and help coordinating efforts of the authors and internal Ernst & Young reviewers.

We appreciate the contributions from all Ernst & Young Quality Consulting Group members, who provided feedback on various drafts.

We thank and are in awe of the incredibly responsive typing and improvement suggestions from Emman Halloway. Working to finish requirements for her Organizational Development degree, Emman epitomizes a major quality improvement tenet—world class quality, productivity, and flexibility go hand-in-hand.

Lastly, for their tolerance, understanding and love when we were writing instead of attending to their needs, we thank our families.

FOREWORD

People have been fooled into believing that quality management is a complicated issue driven by an "alphabet soup" of options and alternatives. SPC, TQC, TQM, JIT, CEDAC, QFD, EIT, DOE . . . . The list goes on and on. It is confusing.

Now, you have a book that has taken the confusion and mystery out of quality improvement. *TOTAL QUALITY: An Executive's Guide to the 1990s* takes the "alphabet soup" and boils it down to easy-to-read, concise descriptions that are practical to use. By presenting the total spectrum of improvement concepts, it has taken away the bias presented in most books that only introduce the reader to one or two concepts. There is no doubt that there is no right improvement tool for all operations and/or situations. The company that hangs its reputation on one is doomed to eventual extinction. Customers go to the very best, and unless you know, understand, and use all the improvement tools in their proper applications, you will never be the best. You may be good, but not the best. Being good, however, just isn't good enough anymore. Only the best will survive the 1990s.

You will find that this is not the type of book that you read and put on your library shelf. It is one that you will want to keep at your elbow for constant reference. As you read it, keep your highlighter handy, for you will find many points that you will want to remember. At last you have a road map to continuous improvement. Plot your course carefully, follow it religiously, and your voyage will be smooth, enjoyable, exciting and, above all, rewarding to you, your employees, and your customers.

Dr. H. James Harrington

CONTENTS

PART 1

LEADING CHANGE

CHAPTER 1

THE QUALITY IMPERATIVE

Ronald M. Fortuna

Quality is the most important strategic issue facing top management in the 1990s. What we mean by quality is more than the traditional notion of quality in products and services. Our definition simultaneously encompasses improvement in cost position, delivery performance, time to market, and responsiveness to changes in the marketplace. It is a bottom-line issue that addresses the very roots of a business, and it requires a change in thinking from the top of the organization to the bottom.

"Quality" finally came of age in the United States in the 1980s after many false starts along the way. Early in the decade, many managers were certain that quality circles were the secret to the Japanese "miracle." A few years later, some were convinced that once they installed statistical process control (SPC)—often erroneously equated with nothing more than the widespread employment of control charts—they could surely push imports to the shore. All too often, top management delegated or dictated implementation of the quality initiatives of the 1980s to middle managers and staff. While employee involvement (EI) and SPC have greatly contributed to quality improvement in many instances, the unfortunate fact is that many companies' competitive positions continue to erode despite the initiation of numerous programs. And, throughout it all, the acronyms keep coming.

So what is different now? For one thing, American managers have spent a decade learning by doing and determining through trial and error which methods and philosophies are the most appropriate and valuable. Through experimentation, success, and failure, they have sorted out the vital elements from the less important ones. By now every manager should understand that quality does not result from a beefed-up inspection corps, nor does it flow painlessly from small groups of "involved" employees like tonic from a bottle.

DEFINING QUALITY

Before we go further, how do we define quality? There is perhaps no other commonplace term more misunderstood by business leaders today. While numerous definitions have been proposed, most can be summarized by one of the following two statements:

1. Conformance to specifications—Quality is defined by the relative absence of defects.
2. Meeting customer requirements—Quality is measured by the degree of customer satisfaction with a product's characteristics and features.

Juran succinctly defines quality as "fitness for use," which encompasses both freedom from defects and the multiple elements required to meet the total needs of a customer (e.g., performance, aesthetics, reliability, and service responsiveness). He further describes two parameters of "fitness for use": quality of design and quality of conformance.

We find it useful to expand the quality of design parameter beyond the feature-oriented concept of "grade" to include the additional design-dependent elements of customer satisfaction, such as reliability, durability, ease of repair/service, and relative cost (and, by association, producibility of the design).

While quality of conformance is of obvious importance, conformance alone does not ensure competitiveness. One can easily imagine a "perfect" (defect-free) product that no one wants. It is, in fact, an enormous improvement in design quality, rather than conformance quality, that has been responsible for most improvements in Japanese products over the last decade.

Regardless of the exact definition of quality, quality and satisfaction are determined ultimately by the customer's perception of a total product's value or service relative to its competition.

THE CASE FOR QUALITY

Before we explore what must be done, let us first consider the evidence pointing to the increasingly dominant role quality will play in the world market in the years to come. To put it succinctly, there is a strong correlation between quality and profitability. Quality greatly impacts both the revenue and cost elements of the profit equation.

A good deal of the hard evidence supporting this correlation comes from the Profit Impact of Marketing Strategies (PIMS) studies. Sponsored by the Strategic Planning Institute, this research program began in 1972. The PIMS database has drawn strategic and financial data from roughly 3,000 business units and has served as the basis for over 100 studies of business strategy. In *PIMS Principles,* Buzzell and Gale note that "there is no doubt that relative perceived quality and profitability are strongly related. Whether the profit measure is return on sales or return on investment, businesses with a superior product/service offering clearly outperform those with inferior quality." In their study, those businesses in the top 20th percentile ranking for perceived relative quality had an average return on investment of over 30 percent, nearly double that of companies in the bottom 20th percentile. Return on sales followed a similar pattern.

Buzzell and Gale assert that this performance gap flows from the benefits that businesses reap from having a higher perceived quality in the marketplace: "stronger customer loyalty; more repeat purchases; less vulnerability to price wars; ability to command higher relative price without affecting share; lower marketing costs; and share improvements." Not surprisingly, the PIMS data also reveal correlations between relative quality and market share and between relative quality and relative price. The relationship between financial performance and customer satisfaction holds true in service-oriented businesses as well. For instance, the Technical Assistance Research Programs (TARP) Institute reported that each customer retained by a bank for over five years equated to roughly $400 in profits.

The recent performance of some Japanese automakers in the face of a very strong yen is a stunning confirmation of these phenomena. Although the yen appreciated by more than 50 percent versus the dollar from 1985 to 1988, Honda and Toyota, both highly rated on quality, have managed, nevertheless, to sell their entire allocation under Japan's "voluntary" export quota system (the Voluntary Restraint Agreement). In 1988, the Japanese auto industry as a whole exported only 2.1 million vehicles, even though the voluntary quota allowed up to 2.3 million. Unlike other Japanese companies, Honda and Toyota maintained a sold-out position through 1988. Although few of their dealers still were able to command above-sticker prices, as they could when the yen was weaker, the actual prices paid for these vehicles rose substantially without an accompanying loss in market share.

The 1988 surveys by the American Society for Quality Control (ASQC) and the Gallup organization also suggest a strong relationship between quality and price realization. Survey respondents indicated that they were willing to pay substantial premiums for higher quality goods over the baseline price for the same goods of "average" quality (e.g., they would pay, on average, more for a higher quality television).

A potentially more devastating consequence to the bottom line is the reaction of the consumer who receives a defective or otherwise unsatisfactory product or service. A recent study showed that, while a satisfied customer will tell a few people about his or her experience, a dissatisfied person will tell an average of 19 others.

Unfortunately, the company is usually the last to know of dissatisfaction. People rarely complain directly to the provider of poor-quality goods and services. In fact, studies suggest that people usually complain, if at all, to their most immediate contact (e.g., a salesperson or service manager) and that these complaints are rarely transmitted further. A more common response is simply to switch to a competing product or service. Typically, formal complaints are received from less than 5 percent of dissatisfied customers. What about the cost part of the equation?

The PIMS data showed no direct correlation between relative perceived quality and relative direct cost, noting that "the greater profitability of businesses with superior perceived quality is typically linked to their ability to realize higher prices while achieving comparable direct costs." This suggests that higher quality need not, and did not, presage higher costs. We can postulate two reasons to explain this. First, for competing products using a similar design and materials, better quality was achieved at a lower cost. Second, if higher quality was perceived due to an inherently more costly design and/or materials, those higher costs would be offset by lower costs to execute the design.

In any event, it is clear that high quality and low cost can be achieved simultaneously. For instance, in a study of the quality of room air conditioners, Garvin found that an inverse relationship existed between the number of direct labor hours needed to assemble various brands and their relative quality ranking. That is, the superior air conditioners required fewer hours to produce. This is certainly contrary to the conventional wisdom that higher quality only can be achieved through higher costs, such as for increased inspection.

This again points to an expanded view of quality as a way of doing business rather than as a tactical objective, where quality and cost are determined long before manufacturing. Research by TARP indicates that only about a third of all instances of customer dissatisfaction are traceable to production problems. In the world-class quality company, costs are lower because customer requirements are better known, reducing the need for redesign and engineering changes and for expensive solutions to customer problems. Designs are optimized before production, further reducing manufacturing costs. Higher quality in the field is not coincidental to lower costs—it goes hand in hand with a low internal rate of defects, scrap, and rework.

SOME MISCONCEPTIONS

The old concepts of quality are rooted in American folklore and have not died quietly. Madison Avenue has yet to catch on, thus perpetuating some of the old quality myths. Who could forget Hanes' Inspector No. 9, for example? More recently, an ad for an automaker showed how Ford "prevents" defects by automated inspection and rejection of a certain component. Another ad, ironically for Toyota, touts the company's product quality by proudly proclaiming over 1,000 inspections are made on every vehicle. General Motors suggests that its improved quality can be traced to a new generation of thinking, more involved workers. (Would you care to buy a car built on Monday or Friday in the Rust Belt?)

They have all missed the point. In the end, the survivors will not rely on inspection, automated or otherwise. Nor will they continue to hope that the last people in the chain, the direct workers, will somehow solve all of the problems laid at their doorstep.

Equally relevant is an anecdote related by an Ernst & Young staff member about a lecture he attended during his graduate business school days. The lecturer, a former treasurer of a Fortune 100 firm, was expounding upon the means of evaluating the return on various internal investment candidates (i.e., NPV, IRR), wherein he declared that "there are some projects which you must make that have no quantifiable return, such as pollution control or *quality projects*." The spirited exchange that ensued between the lecturer and the student, himself a quality professional, hopefully served to further the education received by the aspiring corporate managers in the class. Nevertheless, this myth typifies the old way of thinking, the old wisdom about quality.

THE COST OF QUALITY

Some managers have always intuitively grasped the fact that poor quality is costly and that there is a great financial reward in preventing defects at the earliest possible stage. An executive at Hewlett-Packard once observed, "If you catch a two cent resistor before you use it and throw it away, you lose two cents. If you don't find it until it has been soldered into a computer component, it may cost $10 to repair the part. If you don't catch the component until it is in the computer . . . the expense may exceed the manufacturing cost."

Despite all of the evidence, the executive concerned about quality often faces a dilemma: how to convince the rest of the organization of the problem's magnitude. Frequently, an individual executive at a client company will report that the company has difficulty in sustaining a high priority for quality improvement resources. Other executives simply do not recognize the enormous payback potential.

A very effective way to quantify and communicate quality in the language of upper management, the language of money, is the cost of quality (COQ) concept. Dr. Joseph Juran first proposed this concept in the *Quality Control Handbook* published in 1951, and it has been greatly refined since. Also referred to simply as "quality costs," COQ here refers to those costs incurred because of poor quality—essentially those costs that would not have been incurred if every aspect of a product or service were precisely correct the first time and every time thereafter. The cost of quality allows for the isolation of costs that typically are buried, and thus institutionalized, by most companies' cost accounting practices (e.g., allowances, process standards, and variances).

Most companies express cost of quality as a percentage of sales and divide quality costs into four categories:

1. *Internal failures*—the cost of things gone wrong before reaching the customer. This usually includes such things as rework, scrap, downgrades, reinspection, retest, and process losses.
2. *External failures*—cost due to problems detected after the product or service is delivered. Examples include warranty claims, field returns, product liability claims, and adjustments and allowances.
3. *Appraisal costs*—costs for formal evaluations of quality and for determining and maintaining the degree of

conformance required by company quality standards. These include all types of inspection and testing (labor and equipment), product quality audits, equipment calibration, and operator checking time.

4. *Prevention costs*—the costs incurred for activities undertaken to reduce failure and appraisal costs and to ensure first-time quality. These include education and training, design reviews and verification, supplier certification, and process control activities.

These categories are useful in planning, as well as assessing, progress. It is not only the total cost of quality that is of concern, but the direction and relative percentages of each category as well. Chapter 5 details a method for implementing a cost of quality program.

One note of caution: The cost of quality approach may become an end unto itself if you lose sight of the reasons for undertaking the program in the first place. Protracted arguments may arise over the "correct" classification of costs and about the precision of the cost measurements. Keep in mind that the primary benefits of the cost of quality are its initial "shock value" and its function as a means to measure improvement over time.

The shock value often can be quite high. For instance, a 1987 ASQC/Gallup poll showed that many executives greatly underestimate their companies' cost of quality. Whereas many quality experts estimate that U.S. companies typically have a cost of quality in the range of 20–30 percent of sales, 70 percent of the executives said that they either did not know what their quality costs were or estimated that these costs were less than 5 percent. (Experts' estimates of overall cost of quality in Japan is 5–10 percent). When companies calculate the cost of quality for the first time, they are astonished that such a large percentage of the sales dollar is consumed by quality-related costs.

One final point about the cost of quality. Conventional calculations do not attempt to quantify the impact of lost sales and market share due to inferior quality. While these numbers may be among those things that Dr. Deming terms "unknown and unknowable," it is not unreasonable to suspect that they may be larger than the traditional four categories combined.

QUALITY AS A STRATEGIC WEAPON

All of the preceding evidence reveals quality as a powerful strategic weapon. As such, it fairly begs for strong executive response and involvement in the improvement process.

While many executives may not fully appreciate the true impact of quality on the bottom line, the link between quality and strategic position probably has not been lost on all competitors. The Boston University Manufacturing round table conducts an annual Manufacturing Futures Survey of top executives in North America. In each survey from 1983 to 1988, "producing high quality" ranked at the top of the list of key strategic competitive capabilities needed over the next five years. Ironically, however, it was not until 1986 that the survey showed a congruence between the executives' perceived importance of quality and their stated key action programs for the ensuing year. At that point, quality-related initiatives finally topped the agenda, displacing such perennial favorites as information systems integration, production and inventory control systems, and overhead costs.

The 1986 and 1987 ASQC/Gallup surveys showed similar findings. Surveyed executives chose, by a wide margin, service quality and product quality as the two most critical issues their companies faced in the next three years.

UNIFYING PRINCIPLES

A preponderance of approaches to quality improvement have been espoused through the 1980s. Which approach is the correct one? We believe that no single approach contains all of the keys to quality. Quality cannot be copied; there is no step-by-step cookbook that applies equally to all company situations and cultures.

Despite the bewildering array of *quality champions*, each with a somewhat different message, a surprisingly cohesive set of principles emerges:

- Customer-first orientation.
- Top management leadership of the quality improvement process.

- Focus on continuous improvement.
- Respect for employees and their knowledge; employees are actively involved in the improvement process.
- Reduction of product and process variation.
- Provision of ongoing education and training of employees.
- Familiarity with a statistical way of thinking and the use of statistical methods throughout the organization.
- Emphasis on prevention rather than detection.
- View of vendors as long-term partners.
- Performance measures that are consistent with the goals of the organization.
- Standardization—the development of and adherence to the best known ways to perform a given task.
- Emphasis of product and service quality in design.
- Cooperation and involvement of all functions within an organization.
- Awareness of the needs of internal customers.
- Substantial cultural change.

Remember that this transformation will not occur overnight, there are no shortcuts. It took the Japanese over 20 years to approach, then surpass, the quality and productivity levels of their American counterparts. Dr. Deming cautions that "people who expect quick results are doomed to failure." While many specific projects along the way will yield high returns, the journey to world-class quality performance may take five years or more in a large organization. Figure 1 presents a conceptual model showing four major steps to attaining world-class quality status.

BUILDING IN CUSTOMER SATISFACTION

Once a company accepts the notion that customers define quality, it becomes apparent that the responsibility for quality reaches beyond that of the Quality Assurance/Quality Control function. It begins with a thorough understanding of the customer's needs and largely depends upon the quality of design. Quality function deployment (QFD) is a powerful method that

FIGURE 1
Conceptual Model Showing Major Steps to World-Class Status

I	II	III	IV
Top management awareness and education	*Building a critical mass*	*Achieving total quality control*	*World-class quality/world-class competitor*
Understand need and benefits	25–50% of management committed to quality	All employees in all departments introduced to basic tools/philosophy of total quality control (TQC)	Design quality dominates efforts
Learn and apply:	Pilot projects (limited scope)	Organizationwide commitment	Reorganization around key products/services, markets
Quality improvement process	Education in quality concepts/philosophy (20–30%)	Many cross-functional improvement efforts	Process institutionalized and self-sustaining
Problem-solving tools	Training in basic tools (10–20%)	Suppliers heavily involved	Totally consistent management practices
Statistical thinking	Facilitation training (EI, team process)	TQC promotion organization/upper management audits	50%+ trained in advanced tools
Develop vision, change strategy, plans	Education in advanced tools (1–2%)	Ways of life:	
Form steering committee		Customer orientation	
		Continuous improvement	
		Elimination of waste	
		Prevention, not detection	
		Reduction of variation	
		Statistical thinking/use of data	
		Adherence to best known methods	
		Respect for people and their knowledge	
		Use of best available tools	

thorough understanding of the customer's needs and largely depends upon the quality of design. Quality function deployment (QFD) is a powerful method that many companies have begun to use to help develop products faster, with lower cost and with better customer acceptance.

QFD facilitates product design decisions by giving focus to what is really important to the customer, and it fosters consistent understanding among all functions. It is a planning, communication, and documentation tool that determines where energy, effort, quality improvement tools, and technology need to be applied in order to sustain the overall product plan.

Masaaki Imai, author of *Kaizen,* states that "quality deployment has been regarded as the most significant development to come out of total quality control in the last thirty years." While some American companies refer to it as "matrix product planning" or "strategic product development," the method is based on a structured, disciplined approach to the product development process. This approach begins with and is driven by a thorough understanding of customers' satisfaction with those things that they deem important.

QFD provides a mechanism for determining customer requirements and translating them into relevant technical language that each function and organizational level can understand and act upon. It starts with the "voice of the customer" at the concept stage and carries through manufacturing with highly detailed instructions for production process control or for how front-line employees will provide a service. The mechanism is generally presented as a series of related matrices and charts.

The "House of Quality," also referred to as the "product planning matrix," is one of the most important matrices in QFD, and it usually forms the basis for further planning and definition. It relates market or customer requirements for a product or service to higher level internal technical and design requirements. It maps out what the customer wants and how the company will meet those wants in the following ways:

- Comparing a product or service's current level of performance to the competition.
- Prioritizing the importance of customer requirements.
- Analyzing potential sales points.

- Determining the most important items to improve upon or control to meet customer requirements.
- Developing an initial product/service plan based on data about customer preferences and current competitive status.

A key objective of a QFD study should be to develop products or services that go beyond customer expectations, that delight or excite customers in addition to meeting their basic needs.

The process of accomplishing the priorities from the House of Quality are detailed further using additional matrices in subsequent stages of the QFD process. A simplified example can show you how this works. Suppose that you are a manufacturer of pinball games. While there are a number of things that are important to your customers, let us further assume that, using QFD, it has been determined that one of the highest priority items is the customer requirement that "all of the game features work all of the time." Although you may not be dealing with a "new" customer expectation, it is one aspect of the product that, if improved, will give your games a significant advantage in the marketplace. The structure of QFD helps to ensure that the customers' needs are translated into specific actions that must be performed at each stage of the process:

Product planning	*Customer requirement* All of the game features work.
Product design	*Design requirement* Flippers operate 250,000 times without failing.
Process planning	*Critical part/mechanism characteristics* Coil bracket bend = $90° + 1°$. Bracket metal hardness = 50–60 Rockwell.
	Key processes/process characteristics Die height. Ram force. Die sharpness.
Process control planning	*Process control methods* Check die sharpness every 5,000 parts. Maintenance intervals. Use precision square and calipers. Measure five pieces every hour. Use $\overline{X}$ and R charts.

A potent set of tools for improving the quality of design, often used in conjunction with QFD, includes the methods for design and analysis of industrial experimentation. Frequently referred to simply as design of experiments (DOE), they can improve designs and performance in a variety of engineering and manufacturing applications. Experimental, in this sense, refers to a situation where the experimenter selects factors for study, deliberately varies those factors in a predetermined way, and then studies the effect of these actions.

There are many applications for the design and analysis of experiments, including the following:

- Determining optimal design targets.
- Comparing methods or machines.
- Studying the relative effects of various process variables.
- Evaluating measurement system errors.
- Determining design tolerances.

There are also many different types of experimental designs, which vary by structure, application, and type of information to be provided. Without further elaboration about the methods themselves, let it suffice to say that some quality experts maintain that DOE is responsible for half of the quality improvement results posted in recent years by some of Japan's leading manufacturers. Chapter 8 describes QFD and DOE in more detail.

CONTINUOUS IMPROVEMENT

Is quality improvement a program? We argue that it is not, believing it is more a journey than a destination. It is a process of continuous improvement adopted to remain competitive in the long run. The reasoning behind this view is as follows:

- Because of its strategic implications, the effects of significant quality improvement will be readily felt by competitors. Some of them will respond by meeting or exceeding the new quality standard, making continuous improvement imperative for maintaining a competitive edge.

• Customers' expectations are continuously increasing. By many objective measures, the quality of American products and services *has* increased throughout the 1980s. The number of consumers giving American products high marks for quality, however, did not rise significantly in the ASQC/Gallup surveys from 1985 to 1988. In 1985, 48 percent gave high ratings, while in 1988 the figure was 51 percent.
• Experience shows that it is difficult to maintain a given quality level—to plateau—without backsliding.

There are some fundamental concepts relating to all aspects of a continuous improvement process:

• The plan-do-check-act (PDCA) cycle.
• Management by planning.
• Statistical thinking.
• Standardization.

The PDCA Cycle

The plan-do-check-act cycle is a universally applicable sequence for continuous improvement and forms the conceptual base for the improvement activities of many world-class manufacturers. It is at the heart of all quality-related efforts, from those that are companywide, such as strategic planning, to those of small work teams. The PDCA cycle can be depicted as a continuous wheel, encouraging people not to view improvement as a project with a discrete beginning and end, but rather, as an ongoing series of steps (see Figure 2).

The four major steps of the cycle are as follows:

• *Plan*—Begin by studying an organization's current situation. Before any improvement plans are made, ensure that the current best known methods are documented and standardized. It is imperative to start from a stable base so that the effectiveness of actions can be evaluated later.

Next, gather data to identify and define the problem(s) and to help formulate a plan. Only then can planning be initiated for the desired accomplishments over a given period of time, for what is going to be done to get there, and for how the effect of the

FIGURE 2
PDCA Cycle

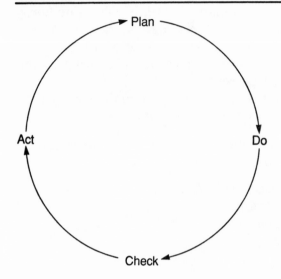

actions planned will be systematically measured. The plan should include specific actions, changes, or tests that are the outgrowth of a systematic study of the probable causes of the problem(s) or effect(s) in question using statistical methods and problem-solving tools.

• *Do*—Implement the plan. If possible, try it out on a small scale first. Insist that all relevant changes are recorded during implementation and that any changes from the planned measures are documented. Ensure that data are collected systematically and in a way that facilitates evaluation (e.g., use check sheets).

• *Check*—Evaluate the data collected during implementation to see if the measures worked. Check the results to see if there is a good fit between the original goals and what was actually achieved.

• *Act*—Depending on the results of the previous evaluation, take further actions. If successful, adopt the changes. That is, institutionalize the measures taken by documenting the new standards, communicating them to all personnel in the process, and training people to the new standards. The new methods, procedures, and specifications then can be replicated in all areas with similar processes. If unsuccessful, abandon the changes or run through the cycle again under revised conditions.

In short, continuous improvement is achieved by "spinning the wheel"—by challenging the standards, revising them, and replacing them with better ones developed by another pass through the PDCA cycle.

Policy Deployment

Policy deployment (PD) is an excellent way to orchestrate continuous improvement throughout an organization by setting targets for the most critical continuous improvement tasks. In essence, it is an application of the PDCA cycle to strategic quality improvement. Policy deployment is the process of determining key policies throughout the company, from the highest to the lowest levels, where "policy" refers to both annual and long-range targets and plans. Policy deployment helps top management to convey their message in a concerted way to all managers and encourages the participation of lower level managers in determining and "deploying" goals. This joint effort is critical to building commitment among managers to attain the quality goals.

To begin, top management creates a vision of a desired company situation roughly five years in the future. This vision usually incorporates specific improvements in the areas of quality, cost, and delivery. The strategy to attain the vision is set forth in a series of annual improvement policies that top management translates at each level of management into specific, detailed actions and concrete goals. The action plans at one level of the enterprise are linked to the objectives of the level above. Thus, the means to achieve a particular target at one level become the end for the level below. This is depicted in Figure 3.

Every person, therefore, must be aware of the four or five key annual policy goals of top management and must be able to

FIGURE 3
Policy Deployment

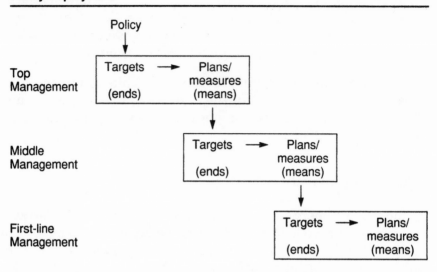

focus improvement activities to help accomplish these goals. Companywide planning and the setting of priorities for improvement are imperative. Obviously, policy deployment should be implemented throughout all divisions and departments, not independently by each department.

Statistical Thinking

There are a number of important business reasons why managers should have the ability to think statistically. In fact, the impact of the managerial use of statistical concepts far exceeds that of shop-floor use of such familiar tools as control charts.

The lack of statistical thinking may lead to problems such as the following:

• Action or reaction to trends that are perceived, but do not actually exist, or failing to act when the data signal a systematic shift. For instance, the yield rate at a critical fabrication step may vary to some extent between one time period and the next. Not realizing this, a manager may mistakenly introduce addi-

tional variations by taking actions when the cause of variation patter is unknown or not understood.
• Rewarding and punishing people for faults of the system, that is, for things over which they have no control because the inherent variation in the system is essentially independent of individual performance. When individuals are held accountable for outcomes of the system, they may begin to manipulate data, suboptimize performance, waste energy negotiating instead of seeking improvements, start to regard the boss as the customer, or begin to circumvent the system.
• Failing to understand past performance and embarking on fruitless searches for a definitive cause for a single observed occurrence.
• Incorrect conclusions about past performance and trends, which can lead to flawed plans for the future.

Statistical thinking has two key advantages:

• Managers make decisions based on facts and data, rather than on opinions. There is a premium on communication with data, and these data are always scrutinized for validity.
• When using data, managers understand that all things exhibit variation patterns. They appreciate the concept of variation and understand its causes. This includes a basic knowledge of probability and probability models that help to explain the data's behavior.

There are two causes of variation in any process or system: common causes and special causes. Common causes are those that are always present and will always combine to exert influence on the variation of the output of a process. Their effects are common to each and every output. They form a constant, stable system of chance causes. Even though individually they may occur randomly or with random severity, the combined amount of variation from common causes is statistically predictable. Predictability does not imply acceptability, but only that we know with fair certainty what the limits of performance will be over time. Such processes or outcomes are said to be in a state of "statistical control." Some examples of common causes in a manufacturing context are machine clearances and backlashes, inherent fluctuation in resin temperature during molding, or the amount of human error introduced by a trained operator reading an instrument.

This concept of variation extends to many types of data. Often executives will expend great energy explaining and reacting to changes in financial and operating data, even though those data are exhibiting variation within wholly predictable limits. For example, there may be great overreaction to the random short-term ups and downs of sales figures, profits, stock prices, or chargeable hours.

Special causes of variation, however, represent extraordinary occurrences in a process. They are not random, and their effect on variation is not predictable. Processes with assignable causes of variation are referred to as being "out of statistical control." Some examples are electrical surges, an untrained operator, test equipment that is out of calibration, or the use of inconsistent methods by different people.

To improve stable systems (those exhibiting only common causes of variation), there must be fundamental process changes. These are generally longer term actions that require management involvement. Some examples are equipment modifications or enhancements, changes in specifications or raw materials, or design changes.

When special causes of variation are detected in a process, it is a signal to react immediately to identify the specific cause(s) and solve the specific problem(s). These are often shorter term corrective actions that can be accomplished by the people who work in the system. Eliminating special causes of variation usually does not require a fundamental process change. These immediate actions might include correction of a faulty set-up, maintenance or repair of equipment, training of personnel, or standardization of methods and procedures.

Continuous improvement efforts are greatly enhanced when management learns and embraces statistical thinking. Managers can reduce the time and energy spent reacting to normal variation, can make better decisions with data, and can more meaningfully evaluate the results of improvement initiatives.

Standardization

Standardization is one of the cornerstones of continuous improvement. The starting point for any improvement effort is knowing where the process stands now. A *standard* is defined as the best known method or way of accomplishing a given task or activity, as well as a means of measuring effective performance. Best known methods can always be improved; however, continuous improvement challenges the existing standards by constantly revising and upgrading them. As they are changed, there must be a great deal of organizational discipline to see that standards are documented, that they bind everyone, that everyone works within the standards, and that new standards become institutionalized.

The development of and rigorous adherence to meaningful standards has many benefits:

- More consistent quality of output (i.e., reduced variation).
- Greater commitment to improvement efforts (i.e., buy-in due to participation in methods development).
- Capturing of individual know-how for the benefit of the rest of the organization.
- Transfer of knowledge from one "generation" of employees to the next; more meaningful job training.
- Transfer of knowledge from one area to another.
- Greater organizational discipline.

Standardization is critical to effectively leverage lessons learned throughout an organization. Many companies only scratch the surface of potential improvements because they fail to transfer or institutionalize improvements throughout the organization after making exciting and significant improvements in one isolated process.

THE EXECUTIVE'S ROLE

A fundamental change in the culture of most organizations is required to sustain long-term quality improvement. In the 1987 ASQC/Gallup survey, 43 percent of all executives rated changing corporate culture as most important as opposed to only 15 percent in the previous year. Executives in larger organizations tend to agree even more strongly with this idea.

Changes in the corporate culture, in turn, demand more than executive support or involvement. They necessitate leading by example:

- Making decisions consistent with the stated philosophy (Do we ship or do we do it right?).
- Communicating with data and using some basic problem-solving tools.
- Developing a vision, strategy, and plans with the active participation of subordinates who must execute the plans.
- Being involved in the activities of outside quality-related organizations.
- Making direct contact with the organization's customers.
- Evaluating subordinates not based on results or outcomes of the system ("How many burgers did you serve today?"), but on their degree of involvement in and use of the quality improvement process.
- Developing a management style that fosters openness and cooperation and that encourages people to identify problems rather than to bury them.
- Displaying "constancy of purpose" during the budgetary process (do not let training budget disappear with every "below average" quarter).
- Interacting directly with those involved in improvement activities.
- Auditing the improvement process and its results.
- Demanding that key measures of quality are developed and given attention equal to the financial measures at all levels, including the board.

The Malcolm Baldrige National Quality Award contains some excellent criteria for measuring the status of quality improvement efforts. The award was established by Congress in 1987 to "promote quality awareness, to recognize quality achievements of U.S. companies, and to publicize successful quality strategies." In 1988, the award's first year, 66 American companies applied for awards that were eventually won by Motorola, Westinghouse, and Globe Metallurgical.

Significantly, a 1988 survey by the G.O.A.L./QPC organization of 130 of the 1,000 largest U.S. companies found that those companies aware of the award, and particularly those familiar with its criteria, tended to report much better results (in quality, cost, productivity) from their quality programs.

Even though the award itself may not be sought, we encourage familiarity with the award criteria and incorporation of them into personal internal evaluation guidelines. Specifically, the award examination items and scoring criteria form a comprehensive base for measuring a quality improvement process. The general examination categories are as follows:

1.0 Leadership

2.0 Information and Analysis

3.0 Strategic Quality Planning

4.0 Human Resource Utilization

5.0 Quality Assurance of Products and Services

6.0 Results from Quality Assurance of Products and Services

7.0 Customer Satisfaction

CHAPTER 2

HELPING MANAGERS GET RELIGION: DEVELOPING LEADERSHIP COMMITMENT TO QUALITY IMPROVEMENT

Ernest C. Huge

INTRODUCTION

Compared to traditional thinking, using the philosophy embodied in quality improvement is a new way to run a company. Successful implementation to the degree achieved by world-class firms requires an enormous change in company culture. This cultural change can only be accomplished by highly committed top management leadership.

Like most everything, there are degrees of commitment (see Figure 1). Many U.S. managers are committed enough to try some projects, but are not nearly committed enough to lead cultural change. Unfortunately, many, in effect, turn the implementation process over to an appointed facilitator and are not involved personally. Some support relaying out the shop floor into cells, but after the physical move is complete, the process stops. Some understand the philosophies intellectually and verbally espouse them, but continue to behave in the same old way.

FIGURE 1
Degrees of Commitment to New Thinking Embodied in JIT, TQC, and EI

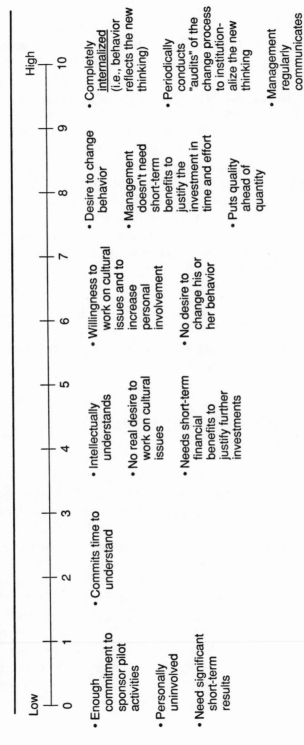

Low | High
0 — 1 — 2 — 3 — 4 — 5 — 6 — 7 — 8 — 9 — 10

- Enough commitment to sponsor pilot activities
- Personally uninvolved
- Need significant short-term results

- Commits time to understand

- Intellectually understands
- No real desire to work on cultural issues
- Needs short-term financial benefits to justify further investments

- Willingness to work on cultural issues and to increase personal involvement
- No desire to change his or her behavior

- Desire to change behavior
- Management doesn't need short-term benefits to justify the investment in time and effort
- Puts quality ahead of quantity

- Completely internalized (i.e., behavior reflects the new thinking)
- Periodically conducts "audits" of the change process to institutionalize the new thinking
- Management regularly communicates throughout the organization what it is doing to eliminate obstacles and improve the system

World class manufacturing requires a "10"

Employee involvement (EI) means to involve all people as problem solvers and solution implementers; everyone has two jobs—to perform their job and to improve the way their job is done. In order to support EI, managers must believe that people have the capability and desire to improve things. Tragically, many U.S. managers do not believe this, and, as a result, EI cannot happen. Without a foundation of EI, other quality improvement concepts cannot be implemented to the degree that world-class companies have implemented them.

To become committed enough to lead cultural change, managers must believe, both intellectually and emotionally, that using these philosophies and concepts is the only way to run a company. In short, they must get religion! This chapter describes the following:

- How managers behave when they get religion.
- How top managers who have religion can instill it into other managers.
- How you can help your top managers to see the light if you aren't a top manager.

DEFINING THE RIGHT LEADERSHIP COMMITMENT

All people want to feel a sense of meaning and purpose in their jobs. Whereas some managers focus solely on numbers, leaders instill a sense of purpose and commitment to the organization's purpose. They enable the organization to fulfill its sense of purpose in a way that meets both individual and corporate needs.

When a leader is committed sufficiently, the values and principles of quality improvement are totally internalized so that his or her behavior reflects these values. He or she is actively involved in cultural changes that must be made. Such a manager has invested considerable time and energy becoming educated about these philosophies and techniques, and leads and audits the process by which the company's thinking is transformed. This individual views the ultimate competitive advantage to be an environment where the creative energies of

FIGURE 2
Spectrum of Strategies for Setting Expectations

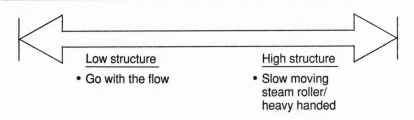

Low structure
* Go with the flow

High structure
* Slow moving
  steam roller/
  heavy handed

all people are better utilized than they are by the competition. The committed leader believes that most people have both the capability and will to improve the operation, and values and deeply respects all people. To this end, she or he ensures that there is an ongoing commitment to developing people as individuals and as a team to accomplish the corporate mission. This manager feels that developing leaders who work at creating an environment where all people can be utilized as problem solvers and solution implementers is the critical foundation for making the cultural transformation happen. Nothing less than a leader who believes this intellectually and feels this emotionally will get the job done.

STRATEGIES FOR DEVELOPING LEADERSHIP COMMITMENT

If You Are a Top Manager Who Has Religion and Wants Your Managers to Get It.

A top manager sets the tone for the organization. He or she must expect that managers invest the time to understand and then try these concepts. The spectrum of strategies for setting expectations ranges from providing a low to a high degree of structure (see Figure 2).

Go with the Flow
Present the philosophies and concepts to the management team in a one- to two-day workshop. After describing what these and

some implementation considerations are, you may ask your managers and their direct reports to consider several places in their organization where one or several of the philosophies can be best applied. Ask them to share their thoughts with other managers at the workshop, then wait and see who wants to do something. Positively reinforce the people who are doing something. Do not waste your time trying to get those who are "sitting on the fence" or who are skeptical. Set expectations by giving attention to those who act.

Slow-Moving Steamroller

This approach is best exemplified by Lew Springer, corporate vice president of Campbell Soups and a tremendous champion of the new thinking. Lew told his managers that the change process was analogous to a steamroller with a roller the width of a room where all the managers were standing. The room had only one door located at one end of the room. The steamroller was going to start at the other end of the room and to move slowly, but at some point in time every manager would either have to jump onto the steamroller or leave the room! Lew did not just mandate it, then stand back and wait for things to happen. He dedicated himself to understanding the concepts as well as anyone. Lew spends most of his time visiting Campbell's many plants to assess and to encourage progress. He eliminated traditional management by objectives (MBO) performance measurements and now expects *improvement*. Springer also holds himself and other managers responsible for creating an environment where people can make improvements.

Unlike Springer, CEO Bob Galvin of Motorola established "reach out" goals, such as tenfold improvements in product quality every five years. (Subsequently, the goal was set at tenfold improvements every two years.) At monthly senior management meetings, quality progress is reviewed *prior to* financial results. After the quality review, Galvin leaves the room to demonstrate his confidence that financial results follow from quality improvements.

Most companies start to implement with a few pilot projects to improve processes. Project teams are usually comprised of nonmanagerial personnel and are led by group leaders or supervisors. Unfortunately, in many companies education and training are given mostly to team members, with little provided to management. Aside from participating on the steering committee, management is usually uninvolved. Consequently, without involvement and with little understanding of what quality improvement is, they frequently do not become *sufficiently* committed and implementation sooner or later loses steam.

Commitment Clearly Follows from Involvement

If people are sufficiently involved with something, they will ultimately become committed to it. If managers are not involved enough, then top management must provide the structure to ensure they are. Top management must expect consistent, sustained involvement. How much involvement is enough? Clearly, the answer varies by individual. Based upon the author's experience, two thirds need to be involved in at least 10 to 15 hours per week for three to six months to really get religion. To ensure this, you might expect your managers to develop an involvement plan for themselves. How, though, should managers get involved?

Involvement must start by developing understanding. One way to do this is to expect managers to read some books on related subjects and to present the essence of the chapter(s) to their fellow managers. Then ask the managers to discuss the applicability of the points presented. Two books that should be required reading are *Kaizen* by Imai and *Out of the Crisis* by Deming.

After this beginning, require managers to receive the same initial education and training given to persons who participate on project teams (at least 40 hours) relative to the basic seven quality improvement/problem-solving tools (brainstorming/storyboarding, Pareto, cause-and-effect diagram, check sheets, histograms, control charts, scatter diagrams). Expect them to apply these tools in some way themselves. After a month, the top managers should hold a meeting in which each manager shares with other managers how the tools have been applied. From this point on, each manager must start using the tools as a matter of course. When managers see top managers using the tools, they will do the same.

Some additional ways managers can get involved at this stage are as follows:

1. Visiting other companies that are successfully implementing the concepts.

2. Problem solving in the new way (i.e., using the tools to eliminate process variation).

3. Becoming involved with another team as a trainer, facilitator, or provider of the resources and indirect support needed.

4. Acting as a positive reinforcer by attending team meetings or roaming around the plant asking individuals how they feel about the change process.

5. Participating in teams to work on communication, education, overcoming cultural barriers, customer-needs assessment, competitive benchmarking, performance measurement and reward systems.

After the management team has developed a good understanding of the new thinking, have the team engage in what we call a "visioning process," an excellent way to develop further commitment.

The purpose of this visioning process is to create a vision of the future state of business after the new thinking has been internalized by a critical mass of the leadership. The vision will define roles, responsibilities, and accountabilities of various functions and organizational levels. In addition to educating and building commitment, having a vision results in the following:

- Provides direction to the strategic planning process; that is, a definition of the future state is required to develop a strategy to attain it.
- Ensures "unity of purpose" (i.e., everyone's marching to the same drummer).

Development of a vision involves brainstorming values, beliefs, and principles that would exist in the future state. During the brainstorming process, do not allow critique of any kind—positive or negative. After brainstorming, evaluate thoughts and integrate thinking. The future vision should be defined in terms of a maximum of 20 principles.

After the vision is defined, a change strategy should be developed to move the organization from its current state to the desired future state. After the strategy is developed, a detailed action plan to execute the strategy must be formulated for the first year. The status of the action plan should be reviewed weekly as a regular part of a steering committee composed of general management. Chapter 4 elaborates on the visioning process.

If You Are Not a Top Manager, How Can You Help Your Top Manager See the Light?

You can help your top manager see the light by describing benefits, especially in those areas of most concern. There is already a significant volume of success stories to draw on from U.S. companies. The best way to communicate benefits is to take the top manager to a company that has accomplished something, then let the personnel of that company share results. Search the literature especially for what *competitors, customers, and suppliers are doing.* This is bound to get your manager's attention. If you do visit another company, depending upon the level of the top manager's understanding, you may wish to preface the visit with an educational session so that he or she will better appreciate what is seen. Have a debriefing afterward to obtain reactions and to provide further explanation. Do not assume people will see what is significant about a world-class company. Carefully orchestrate the visit to ensure that its significance is understood.

Cost of quality data seem to very effectively communicate the financial benefits of quality improvement. Simply put, the cost of quality is the cost incurred because quality does not exist. Cost of quality is more fully explained in Chapter 1.

Cost of quality has not been used in Japan because it was not required to get the attention of Japanese top managers. However, in some world-class Japanese companies, cost of quality has been estimated to be around 5 percent, largely in the prevention category. As a higher percentage of quality costs is spent on prevention, the total quality costs decrease.

Figure 3 shows the benefits that implementation of QFD has had on Mazda versus Ford. Job 1 is the first production model car off the assembly line. The QFD process also enabled Komatsu to bring to market eleven new products in a two-and-a-half-year period, a feat that shocked arch rival Caterpillar, Inc., which had been able to introduce only one to two per year at best!

FIGURE 3
Comparing the Effects of QFD

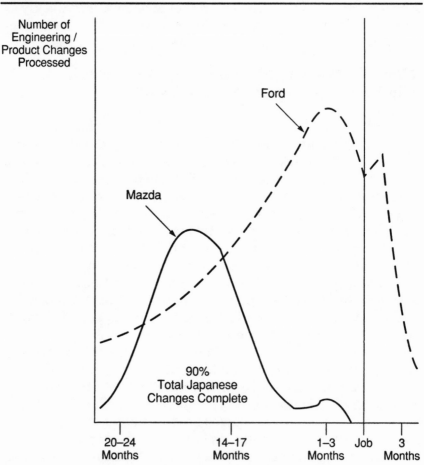

Copyright by American Supplier Institute, Dearborn, Michigan, 1986.

Let the Results of Your Pilot Activities
Show the Potential Benefits.

In many traditional environments, there are situations where a relatively low investment in time and effort and little, if any, capital investment will garner significant benefits. Get started with these. Be sensitive to every opening and opportunity. If a top manager wants an article or a book to read, a videotape to view, and/or a workshop to attend, be ready with recommendations.

If you hire a consultant for anything, hire one who has the religion. The philosophies are so comprehensive that most consulting projects fall under the "quality improvement umbrella." For example, Material Requirements Planning (MRP), cost systems, operations analysis, Computer-Aided Design (CAD) implementation, and automation design must be viewed from under the quality improvement umbrella. Consequently, a consultant with religion can help educate and reinforce the right thinking. It is usually easier for a consultant to talk to top managers about commitment.

If you have started quality improvement implementation and the process is stuck, engage a consultant to conduct an audit of the implementation process. A part of this audit must be an assessment of leadership's degree of commitment. Ensure that the audit is based upon the Malcolm Baldrige criteria.

Ken Stork, Motorola's Corporate Director of Materials and Purchasing, shares yet another approach: "One of our strategies that contributed to winning the Baldrige Award is our Quality Systems Review. It is a rigorous, functional peer review that is a week-long assessment from quality managers of a sister division."

Do Not Wait to Be Told to Start— Do What You Can Do Now!

Many managers see themselves caught in a vicious circle. They say they want to try some of the concepts, but first they need to have the general manager's approval. Unfortunately, they cannot convince the boss to give this approval. The boss has a skeptical nature and is "from Joplin, Missouri": he needs to see it first. There is a company two miles away that is moving mountains. The manager wants to take the boss there to show what can be done, but this other company is not in the same industry and, therefore, does not have credibility with the boss. Consequently, nothing happens.

Even with a boss like this, managers can usually do a lot. Although you probably will not be able to relayout the manufacturing area into product-focused cells, there is frequently enough to get the boss's attention and to pique interest so she or he will want further education.

What Can You Do?

There are a number of things you can do to develop leadership commitment. First, build understanding among the persons who work for you. Then you all can begin to apply the seven basic tools to analyze and solve problems. Emulate the new leadership style, which is based on valuing and involving people. If you have been traditional, leading in this way will increase your effectiveness and your influence. When people perceive a change in you, you will get their attention. The following are things that people in different functional areas can usually do without the approval of their boss:

1. In purchasing a histogram of actuals versus specifications for critical characteristics of purchased materials can be developed.

2. In finance a control chart can be made of a controllable expense. If out of control, find out why. If variability is within statistical control, stop trying to find out why expenses have increased. How to develop run charts to show this is explained in Chapter 3.

3. In production they can stop exhorting workers to improve quality unless there is proof [Statistical Process Control (SPC) proof] that variation is due to the workers; improve layout to reduce handling of documents and materials; and reduce the time it takes to generate an output from beginning to end, rather than optimizing certain tasks by suboptimizing the whole.

4. In quality they can utilize the seven basic tools to solve quality problems.

5. In human resources they can continually train employees to understand other areas and functions so as to encourage flexibility; control chart accidents/absenteeism and analyze the results; and form dedicated service units to enhance ownership and accountability.

6. In materials they can minimize the number and complexity of inputs (e.g., forms, instructions, parts); take "C" items off MRP control; simplify bills of material; and use the cause-and-effect diagram to uncover root causes of record accuracy errors.

7. In design engineering they can seek manufacturing and

supplier input on a new design earlier than before, standardize designs, and identify critical quality characteristics for subsequent monitoring.

8. In manufacturing engineering they can justify equipment the correct way (i.e., return on assets, not direct labor reduction) and begin to standardize tooling.

9. In maintenance, where there is cooperation in production, they can help production operators learn to do routine maintenance; replace tools that wear out on a predetermined basis instead of when they show evidence of wear; and measure up time on bottleneck equipment. They also can use the cause-and-effect analysis to determine root causes of downtime and only calibrate if a process is within statistical control.

Most of these individual actions will not in themselves show large enough benefits to get the boss's attention, but invariably you will uncover some "cherries" to be picked in the process that will show dramatic results. Get everyone involved and hang in there. If you are a manager, then you likely have enough discretionary budget and resources to do something that is significant. Becoming familiar with the seven basic tools will also increase your ability to sell them effectively to others. Explaining to the boss why you are making some changes is an excellent way to introduce him or her to the new thinking.

If you do not feel you can do anything without approval, *then you are probably not committed enough and need further education, understanding, and enlightenment.* Frequently, managers can do a lot more than they think they can. Continually push your perceived limits of discretionary action.

CONCLUSION

In the final analysis, companies do not have a choice of whether or not they will embrace this new thinking and still survive. These philosophies and concepts are simply too powerful to be ignored. As has been documented many times, we have lost and are losing significant markets and, consequently, our standard of living is eroding.

The primary reason we have lost these markets is that Japanese competitors have embraced these concepts to a much greater degree than we have. On a scale from 1 to 10, if world-class manufacturers are a 10, then the best U.S. companies are probably a 6 or 7 relative to the widespread adoption of this thinking. Therefore, we must feel a tremendous sense of urgency. Our most worthy competitors are not standing still, nor will they, nor should they.

When properly committed, the U.S. work force is the best; we showed that in World War II. To be properly committed, though, we must dampen fear of failure, of change, of creativity. At the same time, managers must empower each worker to be the best he or she can be.

Commitment is what counts and must, therefore, be the major concern of your implementation process. Commitment of an organization depends on the commitment of its individuals. The "bottom line" is that, in order to sustain competitive advantage, each of us needs to be more committed than our counterparts.

CHAPTER 3

ORCHESTRATING CHANGE: POLICY DEPLOYMENT

Ronald M. Fortuna
H. Kevin Vaziri

Throughout this book, we will discuss many specific means to help achieve continuous improvement. These means will touch virtually everyone in the organization, ultimately changing the way people do their jobs. It seems a daunting task to mobilize the initiative of people in disparate functions and divisions for a common purpose.

To do this, top management must ultimately draw up a vision of how the organization will look, act, and compete at some point in the future. This vision must not be inwardly focused nor be concerned solely with the future state of the organization vis-à-vis the products and services of direct competitors. Furthermore, once a vision is defined, executive management must find a way to coordinate and channel activity to achieve it.

In this regard, there are three fundamental questions an executive must answer: (1) How will we prioritize the following?

- Success factors for the business.
- Problems to be solved.
- Opportunities for improvement.
- Resources to be allocated.
- Long- and short-term actions.

Once priorities have been determined, (2) How will we turn plans into concrete, specific, detailed plans and actions? and (3) How do we motivate people to successfully carry out these actions?

In Chapter 1 we spoke of policy deployment (PD) as the "best known way" to orchestrate continuous improvement throughout an organization. PD is a planning process for quality improvement that ultimately ties improvement activities to a long-term vision of the organization. Hewlett-Packard calls it a planning and implementation methodology that is "driven by data and supported by documentation." As in Chapter 1, we speak here of quality in the broad sense, far beyond the traditional sense of the absence of defects, "conformance to specifications," or "the best there is." Quality here encompasses not only products and services, but also all of the organization's business processes.

We should emphasize that what we are talking about here is orchestrating change, not planning to maintain the current direction and level of performance nor the day-to-day management activities of the established pattern of operations. Policy deployment is focused on the continuous improvement process and helps to integrate a company's strategic direction and improvement initiatives, even though it does not displace all other strategic planning activities. It emphasizes organization-wide planning and the setting of priorities for improvement. Therefore, it should be implemented throughout all divisions and departments, not independently by each department.

These are the critical aspects of PD:

- Top management is responsible for developing and communicating a vision, then building organizationwide commitment to its achievement.
- The vision is "deployed" through the development and execution of annual policy statements (annual plans.)
- All levels of employees actively participate in generating a strategy and action plans to attain the vision.
- At each level, progressively more detailed and concrete means to accomplish the annual plans are determined; that is, there should be a clear link to common goals in activities from the shop floor to the top floor. The plans are hierarchical, cascading downward from top management's plans.

- The Pareto principle is used at each organizational level to set priorities, to focus on areas needing significant levels of improvement, and to concentrate on activities that are the most highly related to the vision.
- Implementation responsibilities, timetables, and progress measures are determined.
- Frequent evaluation and modification based on feedback from regularly scheduled audits of the process are provided.
- Plans and actions based on analysis of the root causes of a problem/situation, rather than on only the symptoms, are developed.
- Planning has a high degree of detail, including the anticipation of possible problems during implementation.
- Emphasis is on the improvement of the process, as opposed to a results-only orientation.

We will first describe PD at a conceptual level, then explain it in terms of the specific steps involved—from the development of the vision through the audit of the process to attain it.

The Policy Deployment Concept

How does PD work conceptually? In short, management creates a vision of a desired company situation at least five years in the future. Leading Japanese companies are defining their strategic intent or vision ten to fifteen years out. This vision is usually relative to specific improvements in the areas of quality, cost, and delivery. More specifically, we want to identify breakthrough levels of performance in quality, broadly defined. The strategy to attain the vision is a series of annual improvement policies. When annual policies have been established by top management, they are translated into more specific, detailed actions and concrete goals. The action plans at a given level of the company are linked to the objectives of the level above. Thus, the means to achieve a particular target at one level become the ends for the level below. The measures at one level become the targets of the next. This is depicted in Figure 1.

Every person in the organization, therefore, becomes aware of the four or five key annual policy goals of top management

FIGURE 1

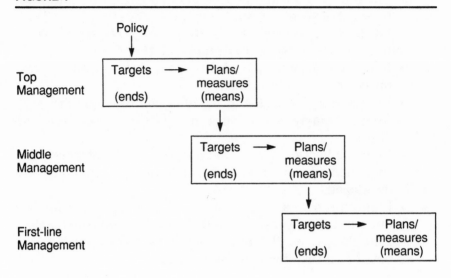

and will be able to focus on improvement activities to help accomplish the ultimate goals. Resources, therefore, are also focused on a few priority items.

In his book *Kaizen,* Masaaki Imai illustrates the PD concept very well with the following example:

> To illustrate the need for policy deployment, let us consider the following case: The president of an airline company proclaims that he believes in safety and that his corporate goal is to make sure that safety is maintained throughout the company. This proclamation is prominently featured in the company's quarterly report and its advertising. Let us further suppose that the department managers also swear a firm belief in safety. The catering manager says he believes in safety. The pilots say they believe in safety. The flight crews say they believe in safety. Everyone in the company practices safety. True? Or might everyone simply be paying lip service to the idea of safety?
>
> On the other hand, if the president states that safety is company policy and works with his division managers to develop a plan for safety that defines their responsibilities, everyone will have a very specific subject to discuss. Safety will become a real concern. For the manager in charge of catering services, safety

might mean maintaining the quality of food to avoid customer dissatisfaction or illness.

In that case, how does he ensure that the food is of top quality? What sorts of control points and check points does he establish? How does he ensure that there is no deterioration in food quality in-flight? Who checks the temperature of the refrigerators or the condition of the oven while the plane is in the air?

Only when safety is translated into specific actions with specific control and check points established for each employee's job may safety be said to have been truly deployed as a policy. Policy deployment calls for everyone to interpret policy in light of his own responsibilities and for everyone to work out criteria to check his success in carrying out the policy.

Before we explain the major steps involved in PD, let us first define a few terms.

Policy—Policy is the high-level objectives for a given year to be accomplished through the quality improvement process. Policies are generally stated broadly and should explicitly support the longer term vision. They are ultimately composed of targets and plans. For instance, a policy statement may include an objective to "improve the reliability of service," which supports a longer term vision: "To be the lowest cost provider of service in the Midwest over the next 10 years."

Targets—Targets specify numerically the degree of change targeted for the year. Targets are the yardsticks by which we measure the degree of success in attaining policy goals. There will be targets at every level of the organization. While targets should be challenging, people should feel that there is a better-than-even chance of attaining them.

Plan—The targets represent the ends, while plans specify the means to achieve the targets. A plan includes more specific actions to be taken. As with targets, there will be implementation plans at each level.

Measures—Measures are specific checkpoints to ensure the effectiveness of individual elements of the plan. Recalling Imai's example, a target for the food-service manager might be expressed in terms of the incidence of spoiled food over a given period of time. Plans to achieve that target might include actions to improve the reliability of refrigeration on trucks carrying food from the kitchen to the plane. Therefore, a measure identified concurrently with the plan would relate somehow to the effectiveness of the refrigeration (e.g., temperature variation), not necessarily to the target in a direct manner.

Key Steps in Policy Deployment

While the specific steps actually used in PD vary considerably from company to company, we think the following six steps capture the essence of the general approach to PD:

1. Develop a five-year vision for the company.
2. Determine an annual policy in support of the vision.
3. Deploy the policy throughout the organization through participative planning.
4. Implement the policy.
5. Audit the process and plans monthly.
6. Audits are conducted by top management.

Let us look in more detail at each step.

Developing the Vision

Responsibility for developing the vision lies with the CEO and his or her direct reports and cannot be delegated. The vision, in essence, is a long-range target for quality improvement. You may recall that we are not dealing here with one-time strategic moves, such as acquisitions/divestitures or product development/licensing agreements, but rather targets to be accomplished through an ongoing improvement process.

As we mentioned earlier, the vision should not be inwardly focused. It should consider the external environment in two ways: through the consideration of customer needs and by searching out the best business processes to use as a benchmark, regardless of the industry affiliation of the company that appears to be the best. That is, you will not achieve a true breakthrough in performance levels if you use only internal benchmarks. Competitive benchmarking, or comparison with the best known in the world, whether or not a direct competitor, is also important in the next three steps of PD. Therefore, we have included a brief section at the end of the chapter on how to go about this.

The vision should not be financially oriented. While attaining financial goals is of obvious import, we have found that visions or mission statements that lay out mostly (and commonly) bottom-line objectives have negligible power to engage people's initiative and creativity. "Increase return on investment to 20 percent" is an example of a statement that gives precious little direction to the organization. It is much better ultimately to tie the vision to customers in some way, to engage people to work together for customer benefit. This means laying out goals for products and services and attendant business processes.

Although developed by top management, a vision is not simply handed down to the rest of the organization. A necessary intermediate step is to circulate a preliminary draft of the vision to all key managers and then to incorporate the resulting feedback. While PD looks, and is, conceptually straightforward, in practice the development of a vision, strategy, and plans is a challenging task. The current literature unfortunately contains little practical advice on "how to." The next chapter does offer such guidance and includes some examples of vision statements. It also explains how to build commitment to the vision.

Determining an Annual Policy

Similar to the vision, the annual policy is also developed initially by the executive officers of the company. There are four primary sources of input to the annual policy:

1. Items carried over from the previous year's policy; a comparison of planned versus actual results for past plans.
2. An assessment of changes or new developments and opportunities for improvement in the internal and external environments.
3. A review of the actions that yet need to be undertaken to achieve the longer term vision.
4. Data obtained from external benchmarking activities, especially relative to total quality control.

Also like the vision, top management must "play catch" with managers through the department level. This involves suggesting goals to them, reviewing their input, resolving key items of difference, then drafting a revised policy statement that reflects agreed-upon priorities for the coming year.

Deploying the Policy

With the overall direction for the year established, each level of the organization must develop plans and relevant measures for activities to support the targets or objectives of the level above. In essence, deployment centers on the determination of the most most important implementation items.

Again, an external focus is preferable here, even at the departmental level. By looking externally at "the best," employees can "be" more creative and adapt/adopt the practices of "the best" to achieve a breakthrough level of performance. We do not mean just the best products and services, but also the best supporting and internal processes. For instance, Engineering should seek to determine an external benchmark for customer assessment and product development, and Human Resources should seek a benchmark for selection and training of individuals. Other examples of things to benchmark include distribution, order processing, customer service, billing information systems, and standardization.

Prioritization of implementation items should extend from top floor to shop floor. This suggests a change in the way quality circles or other improvement teams are chartered. A hallmark of the American quality circle movement has been that each team selects its own theme or project with nearly complete independence. Management is, nevertheless, dismayed when "improvement" proposals are dominated by such hygienic issues as locker-room arrangement or the loudness of plant buzzers. Hygienic issues must be addressed, but should not be the focus of improvement activities. Within companies using PD, quality circles in effect get their direction from the top. More specifically, they select projects that will help their manager meet goals, which, in turn, are tied into the future vision of the firm.

A useful tool to help consider systematically the degree to which the means (plans/measures) will accomplish the ends is the matrix shown in Figure 2, where the various symbols

FIGURE 2

	Plans/measures (means)						
Targets (ends)	△		⊙				
		0					△
			△		0		
							0
				△			
	△					⊙	

indicate the strength of the relationship between a given pair of items in the matrix or, more generally, to what extent the means will help to accomplish the ends.

This obviously looks to be a simple concept. However, it helps to check for the completeness of planning, to avoid duplication, and to examine the interrelationships among planned actions. Generally, it prevents things from falling through the cracks. Any goal without specific guidelines for how it will be achieved has little hope of fulfillment.

When plans have been made in all divisions and departments, cross-functional PD committees review the plans for consistency, then help the various groups integrate them horizontally and vertically. A last facet of this step is to develop the graphical means to track the actual progress of results. Charts can quickly convey on a visual basis the current previous pattern of performance relative to targets and measures.

Implementing the Policy

Implementation of the policy involves the actual execution of the plans. That is, everyone determines what specific actions will be taken in the very near term to accomplish the plans. It involves planning to a high degree of detail, including the anticipation of problems and roadblocks and the allocation of resources to overcome these problems. As in the previous PD steps, we are looking for the root causes of problems, not tending to the effects. Competitive benchmarking complements this process by providing a systematic approach, with an added external dimension, to involve employees in identifying and measuring their contributions to departmental or divisional goals.

This planning should be done with forms with standardized formats. The forms should answer the five Ws and one H: Why, Who, What, Where, When, and How. These forms can also be used to monitor daily events. This type of planning for daily activities helps to avoid the flurry of activity often seen just prior to a milestone date in a plan.

Monthly Audits
Monthly audits involve a review by division and department managers of charts and graphs that monitor progress toward goals. However, it is important that the auditors be more oriented toward the process than toward the goals. Thus, corrective actions and adjustments can be made midcourse, not just quarterly or annually. Feedback should center not only on specific actions to attain planned performance, but also on how the planning process might be improved so that possible problems will be better addressed in the future.

Audits by Top Management
At least once per year, the president and direct reports must personally audit progress. Again, the focus is on the improvement process, as well as on results. The outcome of the most recent audit should feed directly into the PD process for the upcoming year. In particular, it should partially form the basis for the policy development step.

SUMMARY AND CONCLUSION

Taken on its surface, PD looks to be a lot like management by objectives (MBO). However, there are some critical differences. Analysis of these differences also serves as a good summary of PD.

First, MBO tends to focus on the individual person and his or her performance, rather than on a general improvement plan for the organization. Attainment of objectives is usually closely tied to the evaluation and reward system, hence adding a below-the-surface agenda to the process. Why agree to challenging objectives when you may only end up skewering yourself at appraisal time?

Second, MBO objectives are rarely selected so that individual goals are congruent with general company objectives. They are almost invariably made in a vacuum relative to the manager's goals for improvement, if such goals do exist.

Third, the mode of participation is different. MBO is primarily an instrument of management control; while the objective-setting process is intended to be participative, in practice most subordinates end up giving wide deference to their superiors' directions. The objectives tend to be more subject to the system's outcomes, not to individual contributions. When subordinates have at least half of the responsibility for determining not only objectives but also ways of getting there, they will keep trying until they find something that works.

Last, under the MBO system objectives are generally filed away after each session, then dusted off only for the dreaded quarterly (or usually more infrequent) review with the boss. PD obviously ensures much more timely and relevant feedback. Furthermore, PD focuses much more on the process of getting there, with much more comprehensive planning as to how the objectives will be met and, specifically, what actions an individual must take.

Policy deployment is deliberate, is time consuming, and can be difficult. It requires organizational discipline to be sustained in the face of day-to-day pressures and problems. However, the payback from such a thorough and systematic planning is a greatly improved chance for success. We think that you will find it is an excellent way to draw a road map for change.

A Note on Competitive Benchmarking

One way to excite your customers is through innovations. Typically, organizations restrict innovation to their end products or services through marketing and research functions. The processes supporting the internal customers (ultimately affecting the quality to external customers) are not targeted as much for innovation. Competitive benchmarking encourages innovation throughout an organization. Benchmarking is the process of continually comparing a company's performance on critical customer requirements against the best in the industry (direct competitors) or the class (companies recognized for superiority in performing certain functions) in order to determine which areas should be targeted for improvement.

Benchmarking provides a perspective of the degree to which other organizations satisfy their customers (both internal and external). The object is to meet or beat the benchmarks by adopting/adapting the appropriate superior practices. Focusing benchmarking initiatives strictly on direct competitors limits a company's goals and understanding to the levels attained by the competition (rather than on achieving superiority). In the case of public service organizations, for example, such focusing may be impossible if there are no apparent competitors.

Unfortunately, most organizations have extremely incomplete information about who or what is the best. Consequently, most planned improvement targets are set internally, based on past performance (e.g., by comparing product groups, regions, and budget cycles). This results in conservative estimates of further expected improvements. Competitive benchmarking is the creative tool that enables companies to break free of these self-imposed limits and performance. Figure 3 summarizes the competitive benchmarking process and some useful output of that process to policy deployment.

The marketplace is rapidly changing, and consumers' expectations continue to rise. Eight out of 10 Americans now identify quality as equal to or more important than price in their purchase decisions. Only 4 out of 10 felt this way a decade ago. To continue to succeed, companies must focus increasingly on product and service development and on consumer and market research. This requires the ability to focus externally in order to compare your firm's strengths and weaknesses in meeting customers' expectations relative to the best performers. It also requires follow-up by targeting weak areas for specific improvement activities. The goal is not only to attain timely information on high-level measures, such as financial and sales results, but also to determine how these results were achieved and to identify cause-and-effect relationships that can be translated into specific action items.

Given the scope and variety of information available, the process of gathering, analyzing, and disseminating, only internally generated data can be daunting. In large companies, a centralized approach linked to planning may mean better coordination of activities. The danger is that the organization starts to rely exclusively on internal comparisons without developing a clear understanding of its position on key dimensions relative to the competition.

Goals and plans are effective guidance and motivational tools when people are involved in their development and understand why attaining them is critical to the company's success. A decentralized process of information-gathering that draws on employees' input at various levels achieves this buy-in while moving the organization toward a more participative and collaborative management style.

Competitive benchmarking facilitates this transition and links quality improvement to planning activities with this goal: To best serve customers' needs.

The benefits of competitive benchmarking include the following:

- Creating a culture that values continuous improvement to achieve excellence.
- Enhancing creativity by devaluing the "not-invented-here" syndrome.
- Increasing sensitivity to changes in the external environment.
- Shifting the corporate mind-set from relative complacency to a strong sense of urgency for ongoing improvement.
- Focusing resources through performance targets jointly set with employees.
- Prioritizing the areas to work on first.
- Sharing the best practices between benchmarking partners.

Benchmarking emerged as a management tool in 1979 when Xerox Manufacturing Operations decided to compare the unit manufacturing cost and the features of their copying machines to those of the competition. The Japanese Xerox affiliate, Fuji-Xerox, then discovered that its competitors were selling units at the same price that it was costing Xerox to manufacture its copiers. Xerox used these findings as improvement targets. After the success of these initial efforts, benchmarking became a key element of Xerox's corporatewide im-

FIGURE 3
Benchmarking: Output to Policy Deployment

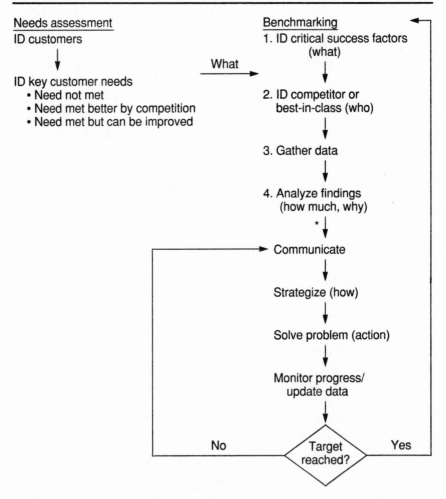

* Output to the Policy Deployment Process

provement efforts in the early 1980s. Several other American corporations have since adopted the process, including Motorola, Ford, GTE, and General Motors. The company's successful efforts in the competitive benchmarking area was a key factor in Motorola's winning the Malcolm Baldrige Award in 1988.

CHAPTER 4

LEADING CULTURAL CHANGE: DEVELOPING VISION AND CHANGE STRATEGY

Ernest C. Huge
Gerald Vasily

There is nothing more difficult or perilous than to take the lead in the introduction of change.

—Machiavelli

Within a context of cultural change, this chapter elaborates on the process to develop a vision, which was introduced in Chapter 3, on policy deployment. Further, it discusses the development of a change strategy to attain a vision.

Although a quality improvement process often yields significant results during its first year of implementation, the crucial transition to a company where the quality mind-set is embedded in the corporate culture can take from 5 to 10 years. Employee involvement (EI) usually is the most difficult and critical component of cultural change. However, the effort to involve employees is well worth it. Many Japanese firms readily admit that EI is the essence of their innovation and productivity. All their employees are expected to be problem solvers and solution implementers rather than passive participants in a fixed system. Rather than issuing a series of commands to direct the activities of lower level employees, managers view employees as their customers and make a genuine effort to address

FIGURE 1
Creating Alignment between Individual and Company Needs

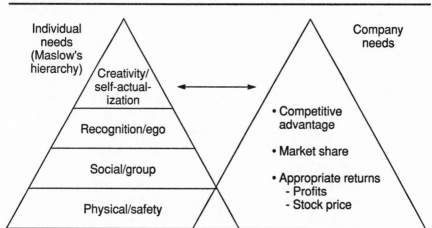

their needs and situation. The employee involvement philosophy transforms the traditional manager from a commanding officer to a mentor and facilitator.

A successful EI strategy requires the firm to strongly uphold certain values and beliefs. Individual dignity must be protected. Similarly, management must believe that most people want to improve the way things are done and that all people have the capability to improve the systems or processes in which they work.

Ideally, employee involvement aligns individual and company needs (see Figure 1). Once corporations begin to fulfill their employees' deep need for meaning and significance in their work, the company's needs (e.g., appropriate returns, market share, and competitive advantage) will be met by employees committed to the success of their work and their firm.

An EI effort will be most successful if it keeps the following points in mind. First, employees need to feel good about offering suggestions for improvement and need to understand that the firm values their insights. Secondly, employees should have the power to take whatever steps are necessary (e.g., stopping a production line) to assure that their process is producing and delivering quality output. Thirdly, emphasis should be placed on the development of people. One way to do this is by appealing to the innate need that most employees have to fulfill a sense of mission, to make a difference. Each employee should have a sense of how his or her individual actions affect the realization of the company's new vision of excellence. Sharing information concerning the company's competitive and financial positioning and market share will help employees to understand the impetus behind these quality-related changes. Fourthly, each employee's job security should be ensured to the greatest possible degree during the change process. Although it may not be possible to guarantee full employment under all situations, such as major restructuring, management should explain that no one will lose his or her job as a result of quality and productivity improvements and that if some positions are eliminated, the people holding those jobs will be retrained for another position. Even when the company undergoes significant restructuring, layoffs must be the action of last resort. Management must explain beforehand all actions that will be taken before this final step.

Managers, as well as nonmanagers, will need varying amounts of time to shift from the traditional "carrot stick" approach to control (i.e., If you do what I want, I will reward you; if you do not do what I want, I will punish you) to control that is provided by a person's identification with the vision.

Paradoxically, in the initial stages of the transition, many top managers will probably need to use the traditional "carrot stick" method with some managers to ensure that the necessary actions are taken to ultimately evolve the organization to the point where the old way is not required. Figure 2 depicts the need to blend the old and the new approaches for some period of time.

Peter Scholtes has advanced a scheme concerning what he calls "the demography of change." The key is to assess an individual's degree of support for change versus the extent of influence that person wields in the firm. It is critical to identify a firm's power brokers and to enlist them as champions of the quality improvement process, while ignoring resistors to change. Typically, a critical mass of neutrals exists that need to be won over. Here, missionary zeal often does not work. Neutrals

FIGURE 2
A Key Leadership Challenge Is to Provide the Right Degree of Expectation

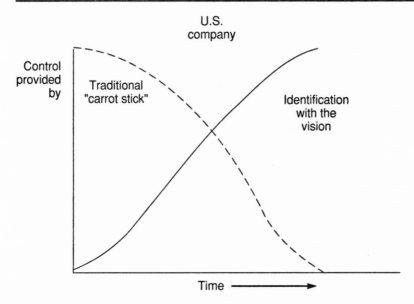

need to express their opinions and concerns and to have them answered in a factual, rational manner (see Figure 3).

A useful motto during the start-up phase is, "Think big–start small." By designing to ensure success (i.e., selecting small pilots with the greatest chance of succeeding) and by enabling these small successes to become a habit, people gain confidence and momentum begins. Management needs to ensure that focus is sustained on both process (doing things the right way) and content (obtaining results). The tone throughout should express a strong, positive expectation of results.

As already mentioned, the change process is difficult. Often high emotional stress and undirected energy are present. Control becomes a major issue, and past patterns of behavior become highly valued. Conflict and resistance can be expected to increase.

Resistance may take several forms. Outright denial of the impending change or focusing on something else is a frequent reaction. Anger and the displacement of anger and fear from

FIGURE 3
The Demography of Change

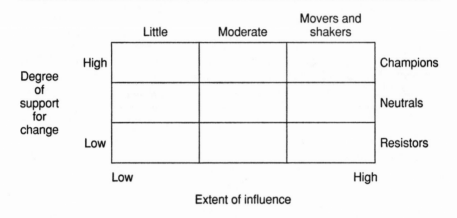

- Identify and recognize movers and shakers
- Work with neutrals
- Do not fight resistors

Source: Peter Scholtes of Joiner Associates 2/5/88

the real threat to a more accessible or vulnerable target can occur. Other forms of resistance include passivity and sadness over a sense of impending loss. These forms of resistance will surface when certainty of negative consequences and doubt about positive consequences arise. Change always implies unknowns that may be fearful.

Leadership should realize resistance will be both overt and covert. However, in dealing with change, a great amount of patience is required. Never force people to take stands. Instead, respect confusion and anger, and allow people to vent fears, concerns, and insecurities. Such feelings need to be treated as legitimate.

To summarize, management must let people know what is happening and why something is happening. Management should provide education and training, should help people identify with the vision, and should set the right degree of expectation. Cultural change is difficult, but persistence and patience will win the day. Leadership sets the tone by being the first to "walk-the-talk."

CREATING A VISION

A vision describes the desired future state of a firm. It explains how the company will work after quality improvement thinking is in place and how things will get done—it outlines roles, responsibilities, and accountabilities. Most of all, it identifies the beliefs and values that will motivate a company's passion for excellence.

According to Napoleon Hill in *Think and Grow Rich,* the basic premise of creative visioning is that a person can achieve whatever he or she can conceive and believe. A vision arises from the hopes and aspirations of a company's leadership. Ideally, it is a creation that is independent of the way things currently are.

John Adams, in *Transforming Leadership,* has pointed out that one of the greatest misunderstandings of what true vision is deals with the relationship between vision and circumstances. Most people attempt to derive their vision from the circumstances in which they find themselves. This seldom leads to a creative act, for the vision itself is limited by the analysis of circumstances, and by the biases inherent in the analysis and is subject to the influence of past aspirations.

In order to generate real vision, the vision itself must be conceived independent of circumstances. The vision must also be conceived without reference to the apparent possibility or impossibility of its accomplishment. Since most people have been trained to think in terms of responding appropriately to circumstances, the unfortunate policy of limiting what one wants to what seems possible and realistic forms a common countercreative habit.

Rather than make up visions of desired results, most people focus on process—methods of acting, steps to be taken, and forms to be followed. The process answers the question, How do I bring what I want into reality? This is a good question once you know what you want, but a useless question until you do. When people substitute the question, What among the available alternatives do I want to do? for the question, What do I want to create?, vision degenerates into process. Upon conceiving a vision, process must not initially be considered.

A company's vision serves several purposes. It provides direction for all actions, including change strategies and plans, and ensures unity of purpose. It also can be a powerful motivator that inspires the firm's entire operation. As it generates spirit and enthusiasm it creates a sense of meaning. It should appeal to the heart, as well as to the mind, in order to reach the deepest levels of each employee's energy.

THE VISIONING PROCESS

Top management must develop the vision because they set the tone for the organization. Part of the process for creating a vision involves establishing a mood for creativity. A spirit of freedom, fun, and play should pervade the undertaking. Often this involves having executives relocate to an off-site setting, close to nature if possible. There should be plenty of quiet time for reflection within a nonthreatening and supportive climate. This generates the risk-taking attitude essential for generating new perspectives.

During the process of solidifying the vision, participants should brainstorm and storyboard their ideas according to major categories. Cause-and-effect diagrams that organize thoughts are often useful as well. Figure 4 uses a cause-and-effect diagram to list the major areas that a vision should address. After brainstorming, the group should evaluate all ideas and consolidate their thinking into no more than 20 statements. These statements will form the basis of the firm's new philosophy.

The mission statement is the foundation of any vision because it gives the company a sense of purpose. If a company already has a mission statement, it should be evaluated. A mission statement that stresses service and nonfinancial concerns will energize people. Although spiritual values are frequently disallowed in business contexts, it is these very spiritual values that are most powerful in moving people to act.

Examples of vision statements include the following: "All people will be utilized as problem solvers and implementers" and "We will invest in the development of people. We expect every individual to spend at least 10 percent of their time in education/training and improving the way their job is per-

FIGURE 4

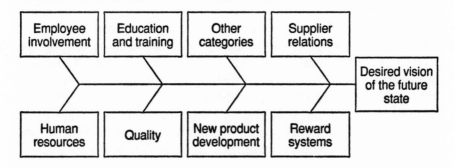

formed." (See Figure 6 for a complete example of mission statement and vision of Ernst & Young's quality improvement
consulting practice. Figure 7 is the sample vision of a manufacturing company.)

ROLLING OUT THE VISION

A draft of the company's new vision should be presented to the
next level of managers after they have gained sufficient
understanding of the new quality paradigm. Incorporate
feedback from these managers into a second draft. The vision
statement should be viewed as a living document and should
be finalized only after feedback has been requested from all
levels.

A change strategy details how the transformation to attain
the vision will occur. It describes the approaches to be used and
sets a timetable for major events and milestones. It should
evolve continually. Management should begin developing a
change strategy by first assessing the current state of the
company, identifying what can be built upon and what must be
changed. The gap between the vision and current state is
gauged, and the means to fill the gap is delineated. After the
change strategy is developed, management deploys the vision
and change strategy through a process called policy deployment
(PD), which is described in Chapter 3.

KEY STRATEGIC ELEMENTS

Several strategic elements contribute significantly to the change strategy's success: building political support among the various constituencies, setting an appropriate rate of change, performance measurement, education, and employment security. Similarly, ensuring individual dignity, using external consultants, setting new policies, and introducing automation must all be studied for appropriate inclusion in the change strategy. The rest of this chapter examines these strategic elements.

Building Political Support

In the process of motivating the company's people, it may be helpful to assess individuals' commitment and influence. Highly influential quality champions committed to the improvement should be enlisted to win over those undecided about the new paradigm. It also may be helpful to cultivate the general work environment by encouraging positive feedback, rewarding enlightened behavior, and acting quickly to quell negative rumors.

It is crucial for employees to see their managers practicing what they advocate, or "walking the talk" themselves. Leadership should recognize any positive accomplishments and should build upon them. Required resources must be allocated to support all change.

Organizational readiness must precede all actions. All participants must also be involved in planning the change. Employee involvement (EI) is a function of the percentage of people involved in problem solving, as well as the percentage of their time spent improving versus maintaining the system. Similarly, the degree of voluntary versus involuntary action affects the planned rate of change.

The company's commitment to the rate of change can be assessed by examining its timetable for major events. If a firm aspires to win a national or international award (i.e., the Malcolm Baldrige National Quality Award or the Deming Prize) and sets a date for that achievement, it is demonstrating a sincere commitment to quality.

Performance Measurement

Before devising new performance measurements or reward systems, management must understand the shortcomings of the current systems. A firm's current measurements should be assessed to determine whether or not they measure outcomes of systems or of performance that relate only to an individual. For example, inventory measures the outcome of a system, but the number of sales calls made by a particular salesperson in January measures individual performance. If individuals are being rated on activities over which they have only limited control, the measurement system is unfair and ineffective.

The process of implementing new performance measurements must include an educational component to inform people why certain performance measurements are appropriate while others are not. Measurements should be changed only after most people understand why they are being changed. Changes should be implemented from the top down.

Reward systems should be both monetary and nonmonetary. Often recognition by superiors and peers is reward enough. More discretionary budget is another positive reward, as is allowing an employee more time to develop his or her capabilities.

In general, performance measurements, reward recommendations, and implementation plans can be developed by cross-functional teams who are well grounded in the new paradigm and who are familiar with the master timetable for improvements.

Educational Process

The educational process for marketing the new paradigm must be carefully designed. Overall, the educational process will follow a similar course in any firm. Competitive benchmarking of how the best go about quality education is extremely useful. How much education and of what type need to be defined.

FIGURE 5
Cascade Education and the Vision

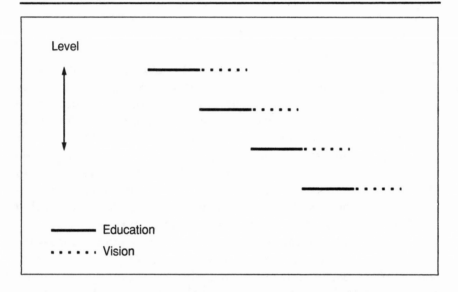

Quality education of subsequent levels of management and employees should preceed sharing the new vision with them. This can be likened to a cascade (see Figure 5).

It is important to decide if and to what degree external or internal personnel should conduct the education. Mandatory educational requirements should be set for each major category or organizational level. Thought must be given to the proper approach for existing employees, as well as for new employees. Annual educational requirements and internal and external certifications for improved capabilities will also need to be designated. Lastly, an educational process must consider input from those educated to ensure that it is continually improving.

Employment Security

The issue of employment security is usually uppermost in the minds of employees. Here again, the existing process should be evaluated. During peaks in demand, a firm should consider subcontracting, instituting overtime hours, and using temporary employees. During times of decreased demand, a firm can accept reduced margins. To increase volume, prices can be reduced to the point where only direct costs are covered. Additionally, more vertical integration and allowing a greater degree of subcontracting will enhance job security.

Some firms have used a profit-sharing bonus to stabilize employment. A bonus can be reduced proportionately for everyone during a downturn, thus precluding the need to reduce head count. Before layoffs, alternate measures, such as across-the-board pay cuts and shortened workweeks, should be tried.

A firm should implement a policy of no job reductions due to quality or productivity improvements; such reduction will only occur in times of severe demand downturns and major restructurings. A "silver parachute" for all employees should be instituted by allocating a percentage of earned surplus for severance. Increased benefits for early retirement can also help ease the transition to a smaller work force.

New people should be added very cautiously and should be carefully indoctrinated into the company's quality culture. Current employees should be continually invested in and upgraded.

Finally, a firm should strive for organizational stretch as a means to enhance employment security. The goals should be lower break-even volume and the ability to increase volume without adding head count. Most importantly, a firm should ensure that all employees understand completely what is being done to safeguard their security.

ORGANIZATIONAL CHANGES

In planning for organizational change, it may be helpful to envision the ideal organization. Given the tenure, capabilities, and will of the current leaders, what would be the ideal assignments?

Gaps between the current state and the ideal need to be identified. Sometimes the availability of the right leadership suggests an appropriate sequence or approach to implement action.

In the process of adopting the new paradigm, a company will evolve from a functional focus to a market/service/product focus with fewer organizational levels. This can be achieved by implementation with new products only and by discontinuation of functional focus as old products become obsolete.

Many firms have elected to use external consulting resources in pursuit of the new paradigm. Often an external viewpoint provides a much needed unbiased view. External consultants' wide experience and knowledge ensure that a firm need not reinvent the wheel.

Employee involvement is fostered by eliminating practices that indicate status differences, such as reserved parking, executive dining rooms, and lack of plant air conditioning. Some companies adopt a standard dress code for everyone including the president. Everyone should use the same entrance. Similarly, having to punch a time clock and to use a public phone tell workers, "We don't trust you." Honda U.S.A., in Marysville, Ohio, represents those world-class companies that have eliminated status differences. During a plant visit, one person asked to see the president's office, expecting to see a sumptuous office because of Honda's spectacular success. Just as the question was asked, the host led the tour group into a 200-by-200-foot room, pointed to one of the many desks that filled the room, and said, "His desk is here. He has no office." Eliminating status differential to this degree is not a prerequisite for becoming world class; however, it is critical that management invest time to address this issue.

Some companies have established employee forums to ensure individual dignity. Typically, a forum comprises representatives from all functions and departments and is chaired by top management. These representatives periodically identify and eliminate attitudes that do not protect the dignity of individuals.

A firm's policies need to harmonize with its beliefs and values. Existing policies need to be reviewed for fit with the new paradigm, and, if necessary, additional policies regarding employment security, educational requirements, schedule changes, and new product introduction should be created.

Finally, the introduction of new technology often is seen as the focus of change. Experience has shown that automation and new technology do not always increase productivity, however. Bearing this in mind, a firm needs to decide whether new technology is designed to enhance the capability of people or to replace them. A firm may opt for slow, incremental improvements or for a quantum-leap approach, where much new technology is introduced quickly. In either case, the company must be sure that appropriate processes are selected.

Orchestrating the transformation change required by the new quality paradigm starts with the creation of a vision by top management. This vision defines the way they want the company to work after the new quality paradigm is institutionalized. The next step is for top management to develop a change strategy to attain this vision. Lastly, *policy deployment* translates the vision and change strategy into action plans throughout the company—from the top floor to the shop floor.

FIGURE 6
The Vision of the Quality Improvement Practice

Preface

A viable economy and continually increasing standard of living depend upon a globally competitive industrial sector. Dominance in many of our industrial markets has been either lost or is being seriously threatened.

Mission/Purpose

Our mission is to help U.S. manufacturing companies attain and sustain world-class competitive stature. Because of the precarious position of most U.S. manufacturing companies, our consulting practice is performing a critical service to the U.S. economy and, therefore, to the entire population as a whole.

Principles

For most companies to become world-class competitors requires nothing less than a transformation in the way the companies work. This transformation will only come about by transformed leadership. We are committed to help develop transformed leadership.
We will develop internal capability in our clients to improve continuously with a diminishing need for outside assistance.
We will promote and create leading-edge thinking relative to world–class competitiveness.
By staying at the leading edge, "we" will be able to add value to all clients, regardless of their degree of sophistication, competitive stature, or internal capabilities.

FIGURE 6
Continued

In order to stay at the leading edge,
• We will develop individual capabilities of community members to the fullest.
• We will invest more in the development of community members than our competitors do.
• Each member is committed to become highly proficient in at least one area of specialty through education, experience, and professional involvement.
Although highly proficient in his or her chosen area, each person within our community will be capable of helping a company make the required transformation. That is, each person is expected to retain a comprehensive view of what is required for a company to be a world-class competitor.
We are committed to long-term relationships with our clients and will not compromise long-term relationships for short-term gains.
All of our activities are dominated by adding value to our clients.
We will always give more than our clients expect, knowing that we will always receive more in return.
We will provide the best quality that is available in all that we do. By providing the best quality in the most cost-effective manner, profitability will take care of itself.
We treasure each interaction with clients and potential clients as an opportunity to fulfill our mission.
Since we operate with a high degree of trust and openness, we will resolve any personal conflicts directly, reserving our energy for productive endeavors.
All community members are expected, to some degree, to develop new client opportunities.
We will maintain the highest standards of integrity. If we can't add value, we won't become engaged by clients.
We view conflicting ideas to be a necessary condition to ensure leading-edge thinking. Being committed to providing the best service, there is no place for egos to impede open discussion. A spirit of cooperation in providing the best quality is highly valued. We value disagreement, but always with the deepest respect for individual dignity.
We will apply internally, to the greatest extent possible, the principles of management that we espouse. We will become pre-eminent in what we do in the eyes of the industrial community and our competition.

FIGURE 7
World-Class Manufacturing Requires a Thought Transformation

Elements of the new thinking:

Quality is satisfying the customers' perceived needs:
• External and internal customers.
Improving quality increases productivity:
• Quality can always be improved; insist on a high intolerance for anything less than perfect quality.
Product quality is ensured by controlling the processes that make the product, not by inspection:
• Design and build it in, do not sort it.
• Reduce variation in all processes.
• Fail-safe the processes.
Quality, product cost, flexibility, customer service relative to the competition can be improved concurrently.
Stop the process when there is a special cause problem:
• Focus on good quality, not output.
• Allow people to have pride in their work; they cannot if they cannot do it right in order to make quotas.
• Never pass on poor quality to the next operation.
Never produce inventory in excess of immediate needs.
Manufacturing companies must become excellent at setting up equipment.
Do not go faster than the slowest link in the process chain.
Ninety percent of the root causes of poor quality are due to the system, not the worker:
• Therefore, management must stop exhorting the workers to improve when improvement is beyond the workers' control.
    Note: There are ways to show whether or not the cause lies with the system (i.e., SPC, the great contribution of Walter Shewhart).
Many traditional performance measurements suboptimize:
• Expect continuous improvement.
Eliminate measurements that emphasize quantity over quality.
The ultimate competitive advantage is an environment that utilizes and develops the creative energies of all employees to the fullest:
• Invest in the development of people instead of trying to automate them out of existence.
• Utilize all people as problem solvers and implementers.
Management's role is to create an environment that promotes this view of the "ultimate competitive advantage":
• This requires commitment to the people, which means commitment to the business in the long run.
• Management's role changes from a commander to a facilitator of a continually improving process to develop people.
Award business based upon lowest total cost, not lowest initial cost.
Develop long-term relationships/partnerships with sole-source suppliers.

CHAPTER 5

MEASURING AND REWARDING PERFORMANCE

Ernest C. Huge

Priority one for top management is to ensure that performance measurements and reward systems are totally compatible with quality improvement thinking. Quality improvement implementation will be impeded without such consistent organizational structures. However, in almost all U.S. companies today, performance measurements and reward systems are very incompatible. More specifically, most U.S. companies have the following characteristics:

- Use many measurements that are inaccurate and give priority to quantity measurements over quality measurements.
- Interpret performance results incorrectly.
- Hold individuals accountable for results, whether good or bad, toward which they contribute, but over which they have no control. This results in individuals who distort and manipulate results, suboptimize individual performance at the expense of the whole, go around the system instead of improving it, and do not cooperate for fear of looking worse than others. Management by objectives (MBO) and Hay plans used by most companies encourage these problems.

- Do not share financial successes and failures proportionately. The most severe example of this occurred when a major U.S. automotive company first awarded large bonuses to its management group, then asked the union for large wage concessions. During business downturns, direct labor personnel are usually the first to go. Needless to say, when people perceive they are being dealt with unfairly, trust dwindles and alienation abounds.
- Rewards are disconnected from business results. The same auto company mentioned previously awarded large management bonuses when profits were down. Gainsharing systems are an attempt to share benefits derived from improvements. Unfortunately, they are largely disconnected from business results.

By comparison, major Japanese corporations measure and reward performance in ways much more consistent with quality improvement thinking. Japanese companies that are successful global competitors derive a far greater commitment to the company from a large percentage of employees, as evidenced by the following:

- An astounding 20–100 suggestions per employee with over 90 percent implemented compared to less than one suggestion per employee in U.S. companies.
- Lower absenteeism—1 percent compared to 2–4 percent for U.S. companies.

World-class quality requires meticulous attention to a myriad of details, which only happens if each individual identifies with the business. Everyone agrees that the key to changing behavior is to reward performance consistent with desired behavior. Many companies have begun to implement quality improvement concepts and techniques. However, the implementation of most are sputtering because they have not addressed performance measurements and rewards. Although good benefits can be derived from these concepts and techniques without measurement and reward problems, how can a company compete with companies having measurement and reward systems that are consistent?

PERFORMANCE MEASUREMENTS

Traditional factory performance measurements listed here are incorrect for several reasons. *Direct labor efficiency, utilization, and productivity* promote building unneeded inventory, emphasize quantity over quality, and overcontrol direct labor—all undermining process improvement and control at the source. Typically, companies use up any direct labor savings with overhead increases. Ironically, overhead has to be increased to work on problems that would not have happened if direct labor's budgeted head count had been large enough to allow sufficient training.

Machine utilization also results in inventory exceeding immediate need. Furthermore, as shown in Figure 1, it encourages having fewer but larger, more general purpose machines, resulting in more complex material flows (i.e., a greater variety of materials flowing through the same machine). This increases inventory and throughput time. Another drawback is the around-the-clock usage of the larger machines, which does not allow time for maintenance.

Budget and cost variances are inwardly focused; that is, although variances are favorable relative to a standard, they can still be noncompetitive. Standards tend to be negotiated to

FIGURE 1

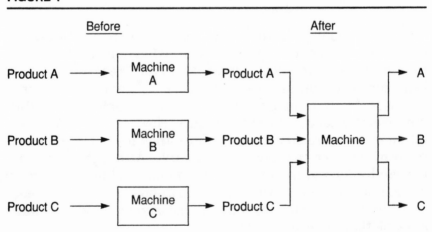

help ensure they can be met. Having parts and raw material variances puts priority on purchasing at lowest initial prices instead of the lowest total cost (i.e., highest quality supplier).

Output measurements, such as schedule performance, on-time delivery and customer service percentage, are valid measurements as long as they are not put ahead of quality.

Conformance to internal quality specifications is another inwardly focused measure. Although conformance to internal specifications is 100 percent, customers can still be dissatisfied.

ENLIGHTENED PERFORMANCE MEASUREMENTS

Enlightened performance measurements are right for a number of reasons. *Total head count productivity* (output divided by total head count—direct, indirect, and administrative personnel) eliminates suboptimizing direct labor head count at the expense of total head count. Enlightened companies also have eliminated the personnel categories of direct, indirect, and administrative for at least two reasons:

1. The distinctions between these categories have become blurry as multidisciplined workers operate product-focused cells/business units. As people become more involved and their capabilities become more enhanced, the distinctions are irrelevant and inhibiting.

2. Categories imply different statuses, which is intimidating. Intimidation inhibits openness, trust, and employee involvement. Top management of world-class competitors spend time designing an environment to eliminate status differences.

Return on total assets avoids suboptimizing machine utilization at the expense of inventory. It also integrates the income statement with the balance sheet, which eliminates suboptimizing one at the expense of the other. Since over 95 percent of U.S. manufacturers have full absorption cost systems, focusing on profits alone encourages inventory buildup (an absolute evil) to enhance profits.

Reduced days of inventory is an outstanding indication of concurrent quality, productivity, and flexibility improvement.

Lead times/throughput reduction is a very important measure for all business processes, such as new product design, development and introduction; responses to customer complaints, and requests. Lead-time reduction is a totally integrated measure; that is, improvement ensures concurrent improvement in quality, productivity, flexibility, and customer satisfaction.

An important derivative of product lead time is a ratio comparing *customer demanded lead time (C) to the combined supplier, in-house, and distribution lead time (M).*

$$\frac{C}{M} = \frac{\textit{Customer demanded lead time}}{\text{Manufactured lead time (supplier, plus internal lead time, plus distribution lead time)}}$$

With most companies, C is usually much shorter than M, causing a company to manufacture, to forecast, and to store finished goods inventory (see Figure 2).

Because forecasts are inevitably inaccurate, they are changing continually; consequently, so are production and supplier schedules. As a company reduces M, the C/M ratio increases and less needs to be done to forecast. When C/M is 1, then all in-house and supplier activities can be accomplished to order. C/M, therefore, is an important measure of flexibility.

Machine availability measures the percentage of time a machine is available when needed. For example, if a machine is required 10 hours per week on average and is available only nine hours, the availability is 90 percent. This measure precludes unnecessary inventory buildup to utilize the equipment.

FIGURE 2

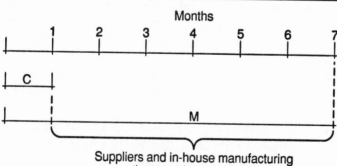

Suppliers and in-house manufacturing
that must be to forecast

Many world-class manufacturing companies measure something called equipment effectiveness for each machine.

$$\begin{array}{llll}
\text{Equipment} & \text{Machine} & \text{Performance} & \text{Rate of} \\
\text{effectiveness} = & \text{availability} & \times \text{ efficiency} & \times \text{ quality}
\end{array}$$

$$= \frac{\text{Planned time} - \text{downtime}}{\text{Planned time}} \times \frac{\text{Theoretical cycle time}}{\text{Actual time}} \times \frac{\text{Processed amount} - \text{defects}}{\text{Processed amount}}$$

$$\begin{array}{llllll}
\text{World-class} \\
\text{effectiveness} = & 95\% & \times & 95\% & \times\ 99+\% = 90+\% \\
\text{Traditional} = & 80\% & \times & 60\% & \times\ 90\% \quad = 43+\%
\end{array}$$

Number of suggestions generated and implemented fosters improvement and involvement. World-class companies implement from 20 to 100 ideas per person, an incredible number when compared to many traditional companies.

Various quality indicators are involved, such as defect rates, scrap rates, rework percentages, percentages of processes in statistical control, or percentages of processes with Capability Index Cpk's[1] within certain ranges (i.e., greater than two), and customer complaints.

Various reliability measures are used, such as mean time between failures (MTBF), mean time to failure (MTTF), and mean time to first failure (MTTFF).

ANALYZING RESULTS

Analyzing results correctly requires an understanding of the nature of variability. Some variability exists in every process. It may not be measurable, but it is there nonetheless. Essentially, there are two causes of variability—common causes and special or assignable causes. Common causes occur randomly in every process and are predictable because they follow a predictable distribution pattern over a period of time ⟋⟍ . For example,

in a chemical process the random variations will occur in the major categories shown in Figure 3.

---

[1]See Chapter 9.

FIGURE 3

Material: The critical chemical
property of the raw materials
will vary around a mean.

Man: Even though a predetermined method is followed
precisely, there will be some variation in the way the
process is performed resulting in some variation.

Measurement: The temperature gauge readings vary from
the true reading.

Machine: The mixing rate in
terms of revolutions per
minute varies slightly
above and below the
target RPM, even though
the RPM setting is fixed.

Method: Although the
setup protocol has
been established, it is
not followed precisely every time.

Environment: Even though the
intent is to maintain a
constant ambient temp-
erature and humidity,
there is, in fact, variability.

Total process: The overall process
variation will be a composite of the
individual variation of the
categories.

Special causes, however, are nonrandom; that is, they are
due to specific, assignable causes not occurring randomly. Therefore, they are not predictable. Examples include the following:

- A bad batch of material due to inadvertent mixing of the
  material with a different specification.

- A substitute operator who has not been sufficiently trained to follow the protocol. A significantly lower yield results.
- The machine that begins to vibrate excessively, resulting in a significantly reduced yield. Excessive vibration was due to a worn bearing, which, in turn, was due to inadequate lubrication.

The critical consideration in controlling processes and systems (collections of interrelated processes) is understanding whether or not variability is due to common causes or to special causes. *This consideration is critical because the strategy for dealing with common causes is different from that for special causes.* Performance measurements indicate variation in the process being measured. Understanding whether or not the performance measurement variation is due to common causes or to special causes is, therefore, essential to correct interpretation.

A fundamental problem with most of today's managers is that *they frequently treat all variation as if due to special cause.* For example, if some scheduled deliveries are not made, in most companies at the end of every month each order missed must be analyzed to determine the specific cause(s).

$$\begin{aligned} \text{Goal} &= 90\% \\ \text{Actual} &= 73\% \\ \text{Variance} &= 17\% \end{aligned}$$

Orders Missed	Cause
Customer XYZ	Parts shortages
Customer ABC	Quality problems
Customer Jones	Tester went down

Supposedly, doing this postmortem will help people do their jobs better. Tragically, it usually does not help; in fact, it usually hurts. A more enlightened way to analyze customer delivery variance is shown in Figure 4.

When actual deliveries as a percentage of schedule are plotted over time, they fall within a distribution with an average of 92 percent and a range of 82–98 percent. Statistical principles indicate the variation shown is random. Therefore, it can be concluded that this variation is due to common causes; it

FIGURE 4
Actual Delivery (% Over Time)

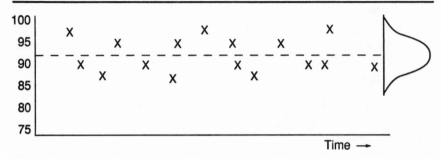

Time →

is a complete waste of time to assign causes to any month-to-month variation.

Another example may help further understanding. With a major chemical manufacturer, a 1 percent reduction in yield in its main product equates to a $5 million annual loss. Consequently, when yield goes down, Ph.D.'s are directed to find out the variation's cause. Because they expect to find a reason, they usually return with one, then impose a process change to correct the problem. Instead, they first should ask the question, "Was the variability due to random or special cause?" If you do not know, do not do anything because you will probably make things worse, not better! *Making an adjustment to a system where variation is due to common random causes, referred to as* tampering *will almost always make things worse!*

How do you know whether variation is due to common cause or to special causes? According to Dr. Deming, you know by "thinking statistically." By this he means that statistical process control theory must be applied to all variability. Refer to the appendix for some very simple rules to use with run charts, which simply plot data over time. No calculations are required with run charts. Because statistical thinking is so critical, Dr. Deming also states that, "The CEO is the first person who should use a run or a control chart." It is much more important for managers to think statistically than for shop floor operators to use control charts, due to the tremendous impact the CEO's decisions have on an organization.

All of the following results are important to management. Managers spend an enormous amount of time explaining these results, frequently seeking out special causes that do not exist.

- Sales
- Profit margins
- Schedule performance
- Rejects, yield
- Customer complaints
- Inventory turnover
- Absenteeism
- Lost-time accidents
- Budget variances
- Machine downtime

Because managers usually hold individuals accountable for data variation, incorrect interpretation can result in an incorrect evaluation of individual performance.

Even if the interpretation of the data is correct, most U.S. managers make one extremely critical mistake—*they hold individuals accountable for major outcomes of systems* to which the individuals contribute, but do not totally control. For example, individuals in the following organizations are typically held accountable for the certain objectives:

Organization	Objective
Sales/Marketing	Sales volume
Production	Schedule attainment
	Direct labor product cost
	Inventory levels
Purchasing	Material availability
	Purchased prices
Finance	Accounts receivable
Engineering	Design release

Clearly, individuals in each of the organizations shown contribute to the attainment of each objective. However, these objectives measure outcomes of major systems that are beyond the control of any individual in these organizations. The individual makes a contribution, yet one cannot determine to what degree. For example, most U.S. companies compensate salespersons to some degree based upon a sales quota. Sales is an outcome of a large system, comprising the following processes and systems:

System Contribution (S)	Individual Contribution (I)
Economy	Salesperson's individual contribution
Competitive moves	
Relative quality (product quality, price, delivery of the product and service)	
Customer's buying cycle	
Interaction the customer has with the various company contacts	
Previous relationship the customer has had with the company	

Assuming that sales over time is a function of only the factors listed, the following relationship exists:

$$\text{Sales} \ = \ f\,(S + I)$$

As Dr. Deming points out, "You can't solve for two unknowns (S and I) with one equation." Unfortunately, managers think they can determine the degree of contribution. Management by objectives (MBO) requires that they do so, which seems logical and quantitative, but it cannot be done. MBO is a grand illusion with disastrous consequences. When individuals are held accountable for system outcomes, they are prone to do the following:

- Suboptimize their performance at the expense of others.
- Manipulate data.
- Waste energy negotiating objectives instead of continuously improving.
- Go outside the system (instead of working to improve it).
- Feel that the boss is more important than external and internal customers.

By having the final say over individual objectives, the boss exerts tremendous power over the individual. In order to look good in the boss's eyes, even though objectives are not met, individuals must spend an inordinate amount of time rationalizing why the objective was not made. Tragically, they are rationalizing something that is beyond their control!

MBO is extremely divisive. Evaluating individuals builds walls around people and around functional areas. Individuals will help others only until they think it detracts from their performance or makes the other person look better. Because MBO is tied into compensation, people know that if someone is evaluated higher, the other person will get a bigger piece of the pie. Since MBO promotes individualism, individuals like it only if they come out on top. However, the company loses overall. Proponents of individual measurements feel that such measures provide a "healthy internal competition" and a "check and balance" a la the U.S. Constitution. Neither reason makes sense.[2]

In order to compete globally in the 1990s, companies cannot afford the wasted energy from internally directed competition. The competitive energies of all must be unified and focused on the external competition.

HOW DO YOU EVALUATE PERFORMANCE?

The fundamental premise of the evaluation is to provide feedback so that the person can improve. Realizing that most quantitative objectives reflect the system and not the individual, evaluations need to become much more subjective. They must discuss the following:

- Cooperation and helpfulness.
- Attitude and enthusiasm.
- Initiative.
- Communication.
- Attendance and punctuality.
- Efforts to improve the system with which the individual works (e.g., ideas generated).
- Tact and diplomacy.

---

[2]For a superb discussion of performance appraisal, I recommend "An Elaboration on Deming's Teachings on Performance Appraisal" by Peter S. Scholtes. It is available through Joiner Associates, Inc., P.O. Box 5445, Madison, Wisconsin 53705.

- Interpersonal skills.
- Interest in understanding customers' needs.
- Responsiveness to customers' needs.

Feedback on the preceding should be provided by peers, suppliers, and customers, as well as the individual's boss. The evaluation should discuss career development plans and status with respect to those plans. Finally, individuals must not be placed in performance summary categories at the evaluation's end, as is done with MBO (e.g., excellent, above average, average, below average, marginal) for several reasons. These reasons include the following:

1. It is extremely difficult to objectively distinguish between people, as is evident in the following performance distribution. Almost everyone agrees as to those who are the superstars (outside of $+2S$) and as to those who are misplaced and out of their element (outside of $-2S$). No formal evaluation process is necessary to identify these people.

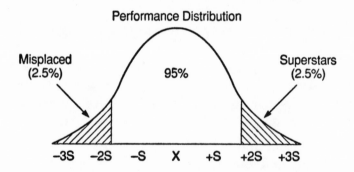

The problem lies in trying to differentiate the 95 percent range.

2. Placing people in categories encourages the Pygmalion effect, that is, when they are labeled, the label tends to stick. A person who believes his or her "average" label, tends not to realize full potential. Ambitious people with a less than desirable label will become discouraged and may even leave the company. When one bright, energetic manager who had been with a company for one year received an "above average" label, he left because in his previous company anything other than "excellent" was perceived as a blackball to promotion.

If, however, there is not a performance summary, what is the basis for compensation? How do you recognize individual contributions?

REWARDING PERFORMANCE

Instead of basing compensation on the summary rating of a performance appraisal, compensation should be based on the following criteria:

1. *The going market rate* for someone with the capability being considered.

2. *Increased capability.* As a person increases his or her capability to do more jobs, compensation should be adjusted to the market rate of persons with similar capabilities.

3. *Added responsibility* resulting from being involved with a greater number of processes.

4. *Seniority* based on the premise that experience brings greater insight into the way work gets done and to the persons who are involved with the work. Compensation based upon seniority also rewards loyalty, which is priceless. Without loyalty, there is little identification with the business and most people contribute little more than what is required.

5. *Business results,* good and bad. When there are profits, distribution must be equitable. The best and simplest way to distribute profits fairly is to calculate the yearly individual bonus based on a bonus factor and the individual's compensation during the bonus period.

$$\text{Individual bonus} = \text{Bonus factor} \times \text{Compensation during the bonus period}$$

The bonus factor is calculated as follows:

$$\text{Bonus factor} = \frac{\text{Earned surplus} - \text{Investment needs} - \text{Contingency pool}}{\text{Total compensation paid all employees (from the top floor to the shop floor) during the bonus period}}$$

For example, if the bonus factor is 50 percent, then the CEO who earns $500,000 would receive a $250,000 bonus. A person whose salary is $25,000 would receive a bonus of $12,500. Most persons who earn $25,000 do not begrudge the CEO earning $500,000, but they do strongly resent unequitable distribution of the prosperity.

Similarly, if the company falls on hard times, everyone will share in the hard times proportionately. When a significant percentage of the total compensation is based upon sharing the business results in this way, then the bonus can be used to minimize the need to lay off people, which causes both the individual and the company as a whole to lose. Compensation schemes, such as this, that provide employment stability have created an enormous competitive advantage for the Japanese.

Employee security at all organizational levels is critical to competitive survival. Turnover is incredibly expensive; the greater the involvement in education and training, the more it costs. Companies must do everything possible to provide security. Although few companies may be able to guarantee employment, compensation schemes that pay a significant percentage (i.e., 20–50 percent) of total compensation as a bonus will go a long way in providing it. Some U.S. companies have implemented these compensation schemes of a profit-sharing bonus. These include Lincoln Electric of Cleveland, Ohio; Woodward Governor of Rockford, Illinois; Herman Miller of Zeeland, Michigan; and Andersen Windows of Bayport, Minnesota.

What about gain-sharing plans? Are they compatible with world-class quality thinking? They really are not for the following reasons:

1. They are based on beating a standard that is difficult to determine fairly.

2. Goal sharing is a group-incentive system. Although group incentives are better than individual incentives, most still promote quantity over quality.

3. The standards on which gains are based are outcomes of major systems that are not totally controlled by the combined work group paid. As a result, persons paid by this scheme will likely receive undeserved consequences, both good and bad.

4. Since they are not connected to business results, gain-sharing plans do not facilitate employment stability. Proponents of gain sharing feel this is an advantage. They reason that it cannot be fair for a group of people to make a $1 million improvement and not get paid for it. Unfortunately, those who reason this way do not usually understand how difficult it is to assign major system improvements to a group. Furthermore, when a company pays a significant bonus in bad times, it usually undermines the company's ability to make appropriate investments and exacerbates the need to make head count adjustments.

Putting aside the consideration for profit sharing, most critics of "equitable compensation for everyone doing the same job" (i.e., with approximately the same capability, responsibility, and seniority) say that "It's un-American, socialistic. American culture is based upon the individual."

As mentioned previously, there are truly exceptional people who accomplish breakthroughs and clearly appear to most others as extraordinary contributors. These people represent 1–3 percent of the total group. In pro basketball, they would be Michael Jordan, Larry Bird, and Magic Johnson—the best of the all-stars.

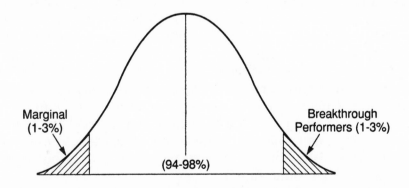

Not only should these extraordinary performers receive extra compensation to reflect their accomplishments, but management should also have a special pool for this purpose. However, do not try to differentiate between the performance of the remaining 94–98 percent; it cannot be done. Instead, pay for differences in capability, responsibility, and seniority. Critics admit this makes some sense, but they insist it is still "un-American." They feel one needs to recognize individual effort among the 94–98 percent.

Rely upon leaders, suppliers, and customers to recognize individual and group contributions in *nonfinancial ways.* Leaders need to provide feedback to individuals and groups every day, but must not evaluate relative individual performance. Nonfinancial alternatives are only limited by one's imagination. The single best compendium of examples known to this author is found in Tom Peters' *Thriving on Chaos.*

Peters believes that substantial, nonfinancial recognition for fairly mundane activities, as well as for truly exceptional performance, is required. The construction of public forums to recognize such achievement is the most important vehicle for engendering the wholesale involvement necessary to achieve world-class quality.

It is imperative that recognition for all acts of special merit be heartfelt. If you do not believe the contribution was anything to write home about, no one else will either. Great managers are themselves most highly rewarded and excited by their people's achievements. Certainly, managers can choose to celebrate what they want to see more of, be it team spirit or customer service. Design the recognition celebration methodically; however, remember that managers must be totally involved and sincere to inspire their employees.

The possibilities for recognition are endless. Often informal recognition is quite enough. Buying pastries, having a special meal at the plant cafeteria, simple thank-you notes, mugs, etc., are all effective if presented with care. More formal recognition events, such as galas and picnics, can be considered after you have successfully handled smaller ways of showing thanks and of engendering commitment.

In short, celebration and recognition help inspire a company atmosphere of participation and total involvement. These recognition events provide a forum for detailed teaching and feedback about why people are being rewarded. They also communicate the spirit, cooperation, and all-hands participation necessary to compete effectively today.

Employee Suggestions

How are employee suggestions handled? Should the individual or group making the suggestion share in the benefits? Generally speaking, suggestions should be expected of everyone and, therefore, should not receive special compensation unless they are truly a "breakthrough" ascribable to an individual or group. The overall aim of the company is to continually focus efforts to attain competitive breakthroughs. Declaring that certain effort justifies special compensation must be done with great care. Thus, breakthroughs will be extremely rare, perhaps one per year. Suggestions, as most things, follow the Pareto principle; that is, a small percentage of the population contribute a large percentage of the total. Persons who are part of this small percentage usually fall within the "breakthrough performer" group and, thus, can receive extra compensation from the special bonus pool.

SUMMARY

The following listing summarizes the principles for measuring and rewarding performance:

1. Do not hold individuals accountable for outcomes of systems over which they do not have total control.

2. Accountability for the attainment of major improvement objectives should be shared.

3. Do not force individuals into performance categories. Positively recognize individual behavior consistent with quality improvement thinking. Suggest what can be done to improve.

4. Build an environment to provide feedback to individuals from internal and external suppliers and customers, including the boss.

5. Compensation should be based on the going market rate, increased capability, added responsibilities, seniority, and business results.

6. A significant proportion of everyone's compensation (i.e., 30–50 percent) should be contingent on the company's success.

7. Ensure that profit sharing is equitable.

Needless to say, these principles are *very different* (and, therefore, extremely controversial) from traditional U.S. approaches to measuring and rewarding performance. This is why world-class quality thinking is essentially a new paradigm for management.

CHAPTER 6

ASSESSING QUALITY

Stephen L. Yearout
Lucy N. Lytle

"If you don't know where you are going, then any road will take you there." Nowhere is this adage more true than in setting a course for quality improvement within your organization. Increasingly, companies are discovering that a thorough quality assessment is critical to the success of quality improvement and that no implementation strategy of the 1990s should begin without one.

DEFINING QUALITY ASSESSMENT

Quality assessment is the process of identifying business practices, attitudes, and activities that are either enhancing or inhibiting the achievement of quality improvement within your company. Ideally, these factors would be recognized and addressed before a quality improvement initiative is implemented. However, quality assessments add tremendous value at many points during the quality improvement process: at the start of an initiative, to guide action; during implementation, to pinpoint necessary adjustments; or at any time thereafter, to benchmark progress.

Benefits of Quality Assessment

During the quality improvement process, particular activities rise to the top of the priority list only if the organization's executive management perceives benefit. Fortunately, the advantages of conducting a quality assessment are immediate, far reaching, and tangible. They include the following:

Supplying proof of need. When an organization considers embarking on a quality improvement program, executives may have lingering doubts and may question the need for such an effort. A properly structured quality assessment provides factual evidence of the company's true state of affairs regarding quality and pinpoints those areas that would benefit the most from the program.

Providing a baseline for future measurement. Properly configured, the quality assessment process produces a benchmark against which a company's progress can be measured while implementing a quality improvement initiative. This enables an organization to monitor results and to identify any necessary midcourse corrections.

Building management support. With the evidence collected during the assessment process, the executive management team can analyze, debate, and ultimately concur on how the improvement strategy should look—a strategy based on fact, not folklore.

Guiding management action. By far the most powerful benefit of a quality assessment is its ability to motivate senior management to identify and to commit to actions required by the executive suite. Typically, much of the assessment data point to systemic issues impeding quality improvement. These issues can be changed only through senior management's actions.

Conducting a Quality Assessment:
An Overview of the Process

The phases of the assessment process include data gathering, data assimilation, management feedback, and management action planning. The data-gathering phase requires particular attention since it sets the stage for the successful completion of the other phases. Any existing quality-specific organizational data should be utilized, and in cases where this does not exist or is incomplete, they must be collected. Interviews and surveys are cost-effective techniques for obtaining an accurate snapshot of the organization's status on important quality improvement issues. These assessment instruments should be designed to ensure that data are collected in such a way to ensure that the findings are actionable.

Understanding what questions to ask is essential to a successful quality assessment. Many organizations have failed in this area because they have confused quality assessment with a more general employee attitude survey. Although employee attitude surveys can be useful and important, they do not serve the same purpose as a quality assessment. An assessment has only one objective: to identify business practices, attitudes, and activities that are barriers to quality improvement so that appropriate corrective actions can be taken.

In order to achieve this, the framework for the assessment must be broad enough to examine the infrastructure of key management support systems affecting the entire business enterprise. The Ernst & Young quality assessment package includes a survey section (comprising a 100-item questionnaire and a section for written comments) administered to a representative sample of the work force and a quality evidence audit.

Quality Survey

The quality survey targets key issues, such as corporate leadership, strategic planning, human resource utilization, and information systems, that greatly influence a company's ability to improve quality. It is designed to present an "as is" picture of the current state of affairs. Because all responses are confidential, employees can give honest answers without fear of reprisal. Since common sense dictates that those closest to a system are in the best position to provide information about it, the material gathered is firsthand and highly relevant. The survey explores employees' perceptions of the state of affairs. It is a macro approach designed to produce general guidelines for improving departments and processes.

In focusing on the area of corporate leadership, for example, the survey examines the degree to which the chief executive officer, chief operating officer, and others in upper management take an active role in implementing the quality improvement initiative. The questions are tailored to elicit specific information concerning the three distinct phases of this process: planning, implementation, and results. Employees' responses range across a six-point distribution scale comprising ratings from 1 (low) to 5 (high) and an NA (not applicable) category (see Figure 1). Typical survey questions include the following:

> To what extent is providing quality products or services to customers a *top priority* of upper management in this organization?
>
> To what extent does upper management actively *lead* quality improvement efforts in this organization?
>
> To what extent does upper management leadership *result* in improved product/service quality?

A related category, this assessing the degree to which unique and innovative leadership techniques exist, asks questions similar to these:

> To what extent does this organization *encourage* reasonable risk taking to improve quality?
>
> To what extent does upper management *recognize/reward* innovation and creativity in quality improvement activities?

In the area of strategic planning, the survey examines the corporate operational (i.e., one to two years) and strategic goals for quality improvement, the process for attaining these goals, and the system for measuring progress. It is an excellent tool for obtaining information concerning the clarity of these goals, the extent of employee participation in goal setting, and the performance trends and results. Typical survey questions include the following:

> To what extent does the organization have reasonable, clear-cut goals for quality improvement?

FIGURE 1

	To a Very Little Extent	To a Little Extent	To Some Extent	To a Great Extent	To a Very Great Extent	Does Not Apply
To what extent does this organization provide adequate documentation (manuals, user guides, etc.) in support of its quality improvement efforts?	1	2	3	4	5	6
To what extent is this documentation updated on a timely basis?	1	2	3	4	5	6
To what extent is information about effective quality improvement techniques openly shared in this organization?	1	2	3	4	5	6
To what extent are you following quality techniques widely used in this organization:						
Seven problem-solving tools (e.g., Pareto diagrams, control charts).	1	2	3	4	5	6
Design of experiments (Taguchi, classical).	1	2	3	4	5	6
Quality function deployment.	1	2	3	4	5	6
To what extent are these techniques being used to prevent rather than identify/correct problems?	1	2	3	4	5	6
To what extent are you aware of how your organization's products/services compare with your competitors in terms of quality?	1	2	3	4	5	6
To what extent is external customer information about quality improvement used routinely in product/service decision making?	1	2	3	4	5	6
To what extent does upper management routinely place an emphasis on quality?	1	2	3	4	5	6

To what extent are your department's mission and objectives for quality improvement coordinated with those of other related departments?

To what extent is your supervisor held accountable for producing quality results?

To what extent does your work group have *specific measurable* goals for quality improvement?

To what extent are your work group's goals for quality improvement *realistic* and *attainable?*

To what extent are you held accountable for producing quality results?

To offer a final example, the survey section on human resource utilization explores areas such as management and operations, employee involvement, education, and recognition systems. A cross section of questions from this area includes the following:

To what extent are you aware of methods or procedures for communicating suggestions for quality improvement up the corporate ladder?

To what extent is your supervisor receptive to suggestions and ideas from your work group?

To what extent have you received the *training* you need to participate effectively in this organization's quality improvement activities?

To what extent do you have the *authority* you need to carry out your job responsibilities?

In your department, to what extent is doing the job correctly the first time more important than just getting it done?

To what extent is there a direct relationship between your pay and doing a quality job?

Written Comments
At the end of the assessment survey there is a section for written comments. This section asks employees to identify three factors or conditions (i.e., clearer quality improvement objectives, more employee involvement in quality activities, increased commitment to the improvement effort by upper management) that, if

corrected, would contribute the most to increasing individual employees' performance. This section is designed to be open-ended and unstructured to give people an opportunity to address issues not raised in the survey. Respondents are encouraged to cite specific examples to support their points. Unlike the survey, which is a highly structured tool for analyzing employees' perceptions of the general organization, the comments section gathers highly specific factual information on an individual level.

Quality Evidence Audit

The final part of the assessment process is the quality evidence audit during which observable data related to quality improvement are collected, divided into key areas (i.e., top management goals, plans, and policies, collection of quality data, or use of quality tools), and rated on the same six-point distribution scale used for the survey (see Figure 2). The audit, performed by quality improvement consultants, serves several purposes:

- Gathering data with which employees may not be familiar (i.e., communications to customers or stockholders) and, hence, cannot respond to adequately in a general survey.
- Assembling information to produce a benchmark against which quality improvement progress can be measured (i.e., the number of customer complaints or the amount of rework).
- Verifying that a company collects quality-related data (and that it is the right kind).

An audit of the human resource area, for example, involves verifying the existence of and evaluating attitude surveys, employee suggestion programs, data on work-related injuries, and related information. The objective is to collect easily quantifiable data that, if necessary, can be clarified by follow-up interviews with select personnel.

Results and Analysis

After the data are collected, the findings are processed to uncover key themes and issues. Ideally, the majority of responses will fall at the upper end of the distribution scale. Those

FIGURE 2
Quality Evidence at the Senior Management Level

A. Top management actions
   External quality activities (speeches, societies)

   _____

   _____

   _____

   Communication to customer, stockholders, supplier, etc.
   (advertisement, annual reports, etc.)

   _____

   _____

   _____

B. Top management goals, plans, and policies
   Written quality policy

   _____

   _____

   _____

   Audit against policy (employee view)

   _____

   _____

   _____

areas where the average is less than a 4 or 5 are targeted for improvement. Figures 3 and 4 present an analysis of the responses and a summary of a company's overall score based on seven key quality categories.

After conducting a preliminary analysis of the data, the key issues (particularly those pointing to systemic barriers to improvement) are summarized and fed back to the management team to guide their creation of a quality strategy and a corresponding set of time-phased actions for its implementation. For example, the assessment process may reveal that a company's policy of keeping workers in the dark about strategic plans, assuming it was information "they didn't have to know," is a barrier to employee involvement, and thus to quality improvement. The consultants and upper management then discuss

FIGURE 3
Test of the Report Format—Baldrige

Respondents: 9

TEST OF THE REPORT FORMAT - BALDRIGE
THIS IS AN ALL RESPONDENT TEST
ALL RESPONDENT - TEST
Survey Dated MARCH 16
Information and Analysis

N	% RESPONSE DISTRIBUTION 1-2	4-5	PRIMARY AREA INDEX / QUESTION: To what extent...	DECILE SCORES (1 2 3 4 5)	LIKE NOW MEAN	RANK	STD DEV
9	0	22	USE OF ANALYTICAL TECHNIQUES OR SYS	M (3)	3.56		.572
9	44	22	23. Info about effective quality imprvmt techniques are openly shared / Following techniques are widely used	M (3)	2.78	116	.786
9	0	89	24. Seven problem solving tools(e.g. Pareto Diagram, Control Charts)	M (4)	4.11	47	.567
9	11	67	25. Design of experiments(Taguchi, Classical)	M (3)	3.78	83	.916
9	0	89	26. Quality Function Deployment	M (4)	4.22	31	.629
9	44	22	27. Qual techniques r used to prevent rather than identify/correct probs	M (3)	2.89	113	.994
9	0	100	USE OF PRODUCT/SERVICE QUALITY DATA	M (4)	4.06		.369
9	0	89	12. Information re quality performance level is adequately communicated	M (4)	4.22	30	.629
9	0	56	28. You are aware how yr org's prod/ srvcs compare w/competitors' quality	M (4)	3.89	72	.875
9	0	56	CUSTOMER DATA & ANALYSIS	M (4)	3.67		.667
9	0	56	29. Ext cust info re qual imprvmt used routinely in prod/srvc dec making	M (4)	3.67	94	.667

FIGURE 4
Scores Summary

	1	2	3	4	5
			Rating		
Overall Score			●		
Leadership			●		
Information and analysis		●			
Strategic quality planning				●	
Human resource utilization			●		
Quality assurance of products and services			●		
Results from quality assurance of product and services				●	
Customer satisfaction		●			

Note: The scores are a combination of employee survey results (rest of the organization) and quality evidence.

strategies for surmounting this obstacle. Periodic quality assessments (at one- to two-year intervals) monitor the company's progress.

Using an assessment framework of this nature avoids the trap of focusing exclusively on quality-related outputs and results. Instead, it forces a thorough introspective examination of the business processes and management support systems through which quality is achieved. Herein lies the essence of world-class quality improvement initiatives.

Key Lessons
Reflecting on the lessons organizations have learned from quality assessments during the past several years may help others to master this aspect of quality improvement. To begin with, quality assessment is unquestionably the most effective way to identify systemic quality problems. For example, in the midst of an improvement project one company discovered that continued quality training would be futile unless the cross-functional

business processes, discovered via a quality assessment, were attacked in a systematic way. After analyzing their business practices, management discovered that barriers existed to applying the quality improvement skills that employees were being taught. Once the management team accepted responsibility for removing these barriers, true breakthrough improvement began.

Second, quality assessment is the best way to involve senior management in the improvement process. In 1986, a Fortune 100 company literally came to life when a quality assessment proved that their current reward and recognition system was inconsistent with and disconnected from their quality vision. This discovery prompted senior management to redesign the performance management system completely and to align it with their quality strategy. Since assessment by its nature uncovers systemic barriers to improvement within an organization, senior management can then become actively involved in leading the change.

CONCLUSION

Companies describing how they would like their organizations to operate from a quality point of view often say that "quality would be a part of our culture . . . imbedded in the fabric of our organization." You can bet that companies for which this is true use quality assessments to continually monitor the degree to which their management practices reinforce a quality culture.

PART 2

IMPLEMENTING PREREQUISITES

CHAPTER 7

QUALITY EDUCATION REQUIREMENTS

David L. Muthler
Lucy N. Lytle

Listen! Wisdom is calling out in the streets and marketplaces, calling loudly at the city gates and wherever people come together: Foolish people! How long do you want to be foolish? How long will you enjoy making fun of knowledge? Will you never learn?

Proverbs 1:20–22

World-class companies realize that all firms have access to the same equipment, technology, financing, and people. The "half-life" of any academic degree is extremely short; therefore, the real difference among companies is the degree to which employees are developed. While most companies strive to improve only the capability and quality of their processes, world-class firms also focus on improving their people's capability. They understand that capable people ensure efficient processes and quality services.

Dr. Kaoru Ishikawa, Japan's foremost authority in the field of quality, says, "Quality control begins with education and ends with education. To promote quality with participation by all, QC education must be given to all employees, from the president to assembly line workers. TQC is a thought revolution in management, therefore the thought processes of all employees must be changed. To accomplish this, education must be repeated over and over again."

Educating employees about quality serves several purposes: it introduces the company's new vision and values and instills a sense of mission; it provides the tools for self-management and for professional development; it enriches workers on a personal level; and it establishes a corporate culture focus on the prevention and the solution of problems and on the continual improvement of performance.

Individuals and organizations alike are resistant to change. Educating employees about a company's new vision of excellence and about the principles that gave rise to it encourages understanding and acceptance of the changes that follow. As old and familiar methods and relationships disappear, confusion and suspicion among employees can easily derail a well-conceived plan. When expectations of workers are evolving, it is important to communicate the quality message clearly and effectively to avoid counterproductive reactions. Rather than fearing the revolution spreading throughout the business, employees armed with an understanding of the need for quality will develop a sense of mission that will be reflected in increased productivity and in a new sense of pride in their work. A powerful philosophy unites people, gives meaning and a sense of purpose to their efforts, and guides decisions throughout an organization.

The educational process provides people with the tools to collect and analyze performance data, to identify and solve problems, to measure results, to develop individual capability, and to cooperate effectively as a team. Specifically, employees must understand how to identify customers' true needs and to translate them into technical requirements throughout the development, production, and delivery processes. They also must comprehend how they fit into the organizational structure and who their internal customers are. They should be familiar with the basics of statistical thinking and recognize the need to make decisions based on facts and data rather than on opinions and hunches. When training individuals for a new job, world-class companies train the person to do two jobs: his or her own job and the internal customer's job.

Educating employees also helps to create a culture devoted to problem solving and to continuous improvement. One of the tenets of quality improvement is that all employees must be familiar with the tools for preventing, detecting, and eliminating waste. This includes the waste of human resources and materials that occurs when workers are not properly trained.

Quality education promotes the development of a new organizational model based on employee initiative, teamwork, and multiskills. Traditionally, most jobs were designed on a specialized basis. This followed from traditional bureaucratic organizational models that assumed work should be divided into specialized functions and appropriated within the bureaucracy for improved productivity and more efficient operation. However, as younger, better educated workers with higher expectations entered the work force, new issues emerged that rendered the traditional organizational models obsolete. The rigid control characterizing these models led to a number of problems, including underutilization of employees, inability to respond expeditiously to problems, high levels of employee boredom and dissatisfaction, and lack of employee involvement and commitment. In contrast, the new organizational paradigm encourages employee initiative and feedback, teamwork, and the notion that workers should learn and apply their education on the job. Mandatory education for all levels of management and workers is the key to realizing this new vision.

DEVELOPING A CONTINUALLY IMPROVING EDUCATIONAL AND TRAINING PROCESS

When developing an educational process, keep these things in mind. Education should be provided on a "just-in-time" basis; that is, just-in-time for it to be applied immediately. It should be built on knowledge employees already have mastered, and a significant amount of education should occur in an on-the-job format.

Providing training to large groups of people for long periods of time (when only a few of these people will be able to apply what they learn) is very ineffective. Training on a "just-in-time" rather than mass basis allows maximum impact at minimum cost. People learn only as much as they can apply without suffering from information overload (which leads to forgetting and necessitates repeat training). They feel in control of the situation, not overwhelmed, and quickly get into the "learn by doing" mode. Education should be an ongoing process, delivered in a series of short sessions lasting only an hour or two each week. An average of 5–10 percent of each person's time should be spent in education and in applying new skills on the job.

Effective training is action-oriented and presented in a way that enables an individual to perform a specific task or function after successfully completing a given module. Because each team member should be expected to eventually master the range of technical skills and knowledge necessary to competently perform each function within the parameters of his or her work team, the bulk of training should be related directly to the jobs at hand.

The key advantage of job-specific training is that participants instantly recognize the relevance of the concepts, which leads to direct application of the new methods. Transferring the skills learned in the training program to their work reinforces the learning process and thus increases the probability of a permanent change in their skill set.

The sooner the learning can be applied on the job, the better. Typically, if the concepts are not used within two weeks, the participants only remember the "buzz words" and cannot competently apply the skills.

Keeping in mind the "just-in-time" philosophy, management should pull the use of key concepts through the organization; that is, each organizational level pulls the concept through their direct reports by expecting its use. For example, even though all the managers and supervisors at Ford Motor Company had been trained in basic problem-solving concepts and statistical process control, during meetings held to discuss quality and productivity problems with the launch of a new car line, a vice-president noticed these managers were, in times of pressure, deserting these new concepts and reverting to their old way of doing things.

Accordingly, during a presentation by one manager, the vice-president asked to see one of the basic tools, a Pareto analysis. The manager was embarrassed because he did not have what the boss wanted. When the other managers made their presentations the following week, they all had a Pareto analysis. The vice-president then asked to see their cause-and-effect diagrams. Once again, the managers were embarrassed. The next week, of course, they all had a Pareto analysis and a cause-and-effect diagram. The point is that in order to get the information the vice president requested, the managers had to use these tools in their reports and, to require them, in turn, from the people they supervised. Thus the problem-solving methodologies were pulled through the system.

CUSTOMIZING COURSE CONTENT

There are at least four different audiences for quality education in a company: executives, middle managers, supervisors (team leaders), and workers (who make up the bulk of team members). The educational process should be customized for each of these audiences.

Regardless of class composition, all education and training programs should begin with a clear set of learning and/or behavioral change objectives. These objectives should be specifically stated and documented in performance results terms. Classroom and on-the-job learning should be supplemented by a self-study component. In general, the educational process should provide participants with the following:

- The tools for self-correction and self-monitoring.
- The reinforcement for applying new concepts and skills effectively.
- The motivation to continue these changes into the future.
- The expectation to contribute to the improvement of the training process itself.

W. Edwards Deming asserts that as much as 94 percent of a company's problems can be corrected only by management, who traditionally have the sole authority to improve the system. It is unfair to blame employees for defective work or substandard performance if they are untrained or must rely on faulty equipment. "Workers work in the system; managers work on the system" is a familiar phrase. Insofar as it is true under the new quality paradigm, managers must strive to create a system that fosters communication, initiative, team spirit, and open discussion of existing problems coupled with suggestions for improvement. Accordingly, education aimed at upper management should emphasize developing skills in mentoring, coaching, and supporting quality improvement initiatives. Executives should be familiar with statistical methods and should feel comfortable assessing the company's quality status.

As new self-managed and semiautonomous work teams assume some of the functions previously belonging to supervisors and middle managers, the latter may feel threatened by the erosion of their traditional roles. They are now asked to approach their work by functioning as coaches, planners, and facilitators supporting the work groups' efforts as opposed to controlling them directly. This change to a more self-directed system is one of the most difficult cultural changes a company must make. Rather than making all the decisions and telling people what to do, managers function as facilitators of a process that allows the creative energies of all employees, including nonsupervisory personnel, to be utilized to the fullest. Many managers will require a significant amount of education and psychological support to ease them through this transition. Appropriate courses for middle managers include participative management, group dynamics (including role-playing exercises), and basic statistical processes. Because these managers will be responsible for training supervisors to be team leaders, they also should take a "train the trainer" class to equip them with the necessary skills to guide maximum performance from their people.

Educating team leaders, particularly during the initial transition phase as a company adjusts to its new quality mind-set, is of key importance because their actions and decisions will have a tremendous impact on individual employees' morale. Team leaders represent to the workers the day-in-day-out reality of the quality process. In addition to being technically competent, they must also be well versed in such topics as leadership skills, customer service, identifying and solving problems, group dynamics (especially the creation of a high-performing unit), fostering creativity, and communication skills. Furthermore, because they will be working in a semiautonomous environment, they should have special training in self-management and in statistical thinking. In particular, they should understand what constitutes appropriate standards, recognize variations in these standards, and address the causes of these problems.

Training for lower level team members should provide them with methods to improve their specific technical and/or interpersonal skills (the relative importance of which depends upon the nature of their job) and should help them to develop skills in statistical problem analysis, experimentation, making and justifying proposals for changes and improvements, group dynamics, self-management, and leadership.

During problem-solving training exercises, each team should be assigned a project. This allows the team to apply the acquired techniques (i.e., data collection, data analysis, and cause-and-effect analysis, etc.) under actual job conditions. Applying these concepts to real world situations provides greater utility to adult learners who desire the following:

- To apply what they learn as soon as possible.
- To use the concepts to help them to improve.

The matrix shown in Figure 1 suggests the types of topics a basic quality training program should cover. Remember the specific needs of your particular industry while continually developing courses to improve and upgrade all employees.

In addition to in-house education and training, there are a number of excellent external sources of information. A continuously improving education process must regularly review and integrate appropriate content from these external sources.

To this end, we strongly endorse the Association for Manufacturing Excellence (AME) of West Pallatine, Illinois. AME's two-day workshops, which are conducted at companies that

FIGURE 1
The Quality Education Matrix

	Executives	Middle Managers	Engineers	Supervisors	Workers
Quality improvement overview	X	X	X	X	X
Employee involvement	X	X	X	X	X
Leadership/ facilitator workshop	X	X	X	X	
Team building	X	X	X	X	X
Creative thinking	X	X	X	X	X
Supplier management	X	X	X		
Setup reduction and cellular processes		X	X	X	X
Problem solving—basic	X	X	X	X	X
Problem solving— advanced SPC	X	X	X	X	X
Problem solving—train the trainer		X		X	X
Design of experiments		X	X	X	X
Total quality control audit	X	X			
Competitive benchmarking	X	X	X		
Statistical thinking (how to understand variability and the correct approach to reducing it)	X	X	X	X	X
Quality function deployment	X	X	X	X	
Total productive maintenance	X	X	X	X	X
General business perspective				X	X
Parameter design using Taguchi methods			X		
Policy deployment	X	X	X	X	

are deluged by requests for plant visits, and usually only allow visits by customers and suppliers, are especially noteworthy.

The usual workshop format allows participants to break-out into groups to assess the company's consistency with world-class principles, share the assessment with the host company, and have the host company share its reaction to the assessment with participants. It's an excellent learning opportunity.

CONCLUSION

Unlike many of our competitors, most American businesses are exceedingly pinch-penny when it comes to employee development. In the companies outperforming us in the world market, education is practically a corporate obsession. Not surprisingly then, given this country's lack of attention to this issue, insufficient employee education is one of the major stumbling blocks encountered by companies launching *quality improvement efforts*. All of an organization's levels and functions should receive some type of ongoing education and training. If only a few employees have the tools to improve the system, a significant untapped resource exists—one that can be developed and mined by education.

In particular, many companies refuse to invest in training not directly impacting an employee's job performance. They reason that better educated employees will leave the firm for higher paying jobs. We believe this is faulty logic and a classic example of the damage that arises from a short-term business perspective. Only by investing in education and training can an environment be created where the best will want to stay. World class firms understand this. For example, in 1988 Motorola spent $50 million educating its employees and suppliers.

Obviously, education and training programs require a significant investment in time, capital, and human resources. People must be trained to use these new skills, given time to absorb them, then presented with opportunities to apply them. It may take a company as long as five years to institutionalize a culture devoted to continuous improvement. The ultimate goal should be to involve 100 percent of all personnel to improve the way things are done at least 5–10 percent of their time. World-class companies invest significantly more resources in education and training than their competition and view expenditures in education/training as a percentage of sales as a critical competitive benchmark.

Since it requires so much effort to set up such a program and no one is promising overnight miracles, why bother? Can we not achieve the same results (increased productivity and quality, improved employee morale and initiative, decreased waste and cost) without going to all this trouble? The answer in a word is no. Quality improvement, the buzzword of the 1980s, is the survival imperative of the 1990s. No company can hope to sustain a successful quality improvement process without investing in education and training. Doubting Thomases have only to consider firms like Ford, Walt Disney, and Motorola to see the far-reaching effects of comprehensive training programs in action. It is meaningless, if not obviously counterproductive, to hang up posters demanding new levels of productivity without providing people with the tools and information to achieve them. In this case, exhortation is demeaning.

In one important sense, however, training takes place in all organizations. Even though no formal process may exist, there always will be informal quality training. This informal training consists of the actions and decisions occurring daily on the job. Management's true attitude toward quality and customer satisfaction is drilled into employees every day by the way they are told to handle rejects, rework, and other problems. When materials that do not meet specifications are routinely accepted or customers are treated rudely, employees learn firsthand they only have to pay lip service to quality in their organization.

Unfortunately, even among those firms committed to the educational process, a tendency exists to give priority to "hard" investments in equipment and tooling, shown on the balance sheet as assets, over "soft" investments in education and training, which appear as an expense on the income statement. You can't see education and training on the balance sheet, only as an expense on the income statement. Consequently, when times are difficult, education is often the first item cut from the budget in order to retain short-term profits.

For maximum benefit, the process of continuous learning must be institutionalized in the following ways:

- Learning should be a part of every individual's professional objectives.
- "Train the trainer" programs should create in-house experts capable of designing and delivering courses that would otherwise require professional educators. Involve as many people as trainers as possible, for these reasons: Trainers learn more than students, and selecting people to be trainers is an excellent way to recognize their competency.
- Peers should assess one another's performance.
- The training program should be continually improved based on feedback from the customers of the process—the trainees.

The creative energies of all employees must be utilized in a successful *quality improvement program*. Innovation and creativity are the lifeblood of a firm's existence and the source of future profits. They germinate only in the fertile soil of the human mind. Thoreau once observed that "People seldom hit what they do not aim at." Quality is the target; education gives people the tools with which to take aim. Those companies that give their employees the correct tools via education will consistently hit the bull's eye and be the leaders of tomorrow.

CHAPTER 8

QUALITY OF DESIGN

Ronald M. Fortuna

Few people understand what the *total* means in total quality control (TQC). Many view it as a broad manufacturing level quality improvement effort nearly synonymous with statistical process control (SPC). To be effective, TQC must have much more breadth and depth; it should cut across functional lines and begin long before a product is manufactured or a service is offered. The greatest leverage from an investment in quality improvement comes from improving the quality of design. Executives, however, have received relatively little guidance in the how-to aspects. This chapter discusses quality function deployment (QFD) and the Taguchi methods, technologies that many companies use to design more competitive products in less time, at lower cost, and with higher quality.

QFD addresses the need to start the design process with clear objectives for a product—objectives that if met will not only satisfy the customers' wants, but also actually excite or delight them. QFD also emphasizes the need to know as much as possible about a product before it is introduced to the manufacturing process.

As observed by Dr. Kaoru Ishikawa, the world-renowned quality expert, we are seeing quality activities evolve into a new generation. The first two generations, inspection and manufacturing process control, are gradually giving way to a third— product and process design improvements (see Figure 1). In

FIGURE 1
Evolution of Quality Control Activities

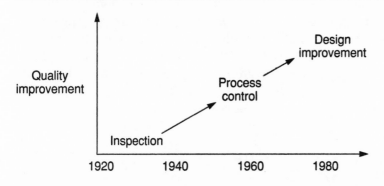

other words, many companies are moving from manufacturing process quality control to product development quality control. QFD is at the forefront of this movement.

RELIANCE ON SPC

Companies should undertake SPC to prevent defects and to improve quality by reducing variation. To that end, many have achieved remarkable improvements in quality and productivity. SPC is a preventive measure, but only to a point. It addresses only the variation owing to the many variables in the production process itself. In a broader sense, it is still reactive in nature and represents after-the-fact problem solving; that is, SPC involves fixing what is wrong and attempting to reduce variation after a product has been released for production. Prevention and reduction of variation, however, can and should begin much earlier in the life of a product.

QFD GETS THE PRODUCT AND PROCESS CORRECT FROM THE OUTSET

Quality function deployment is aimed at detecting and solving quality problems at a much earlier stage than SPC—getting the product and process correct from the outset. It is easier and less costly to correct a defect immediately after it occurs during manufacture; it is even more beneficial to improve product and process design before manufacture. For example, protection against environmental variables and product deterioration can be built into a product at the design stage. Furthermore, optimization during the product and process design is becoming more important in determining the quality and performance variation and manufacturing cost of a product.

QFD: TRANSLATING THE VOICE OF THE CUSTOMER

We know by experience that the product development process is rarely the same for any two products, causing longer design cycles, more product problems, and higher costs. One key to shortening the process and to producing competitively superior, more producible designs is to better define the product and to better document the design process. Although it takes longer to define the product using QFD, total design time is reduced because priorities are focused early and because documentation and communication are improved. Through the use of some structured planning tools, a discipline is introduced to the process. The net result is elimination of much redesign on critical items and a great reduction in overall engineering changes.

First used by Mitsubishi's Kobe Shipyards beginning in the late 1960s, the discipline and structure of QFD are a natural for product development. They solve many problems, such as shared responsibilities, interpretation differences, long development cycles, suboptimization, and personnel changes. Multifunctional teams put much of the data and reasoning behind product and process decisions on visual documents, which help to communicate vital information to others involved in the process.

Although many definitions of QFD are possible, the following captures the essence of the concept for our purposes: QFD is a means of ensuring that customer requirements (needs, wants, demands) are accurately translated into relevant technical requirements throughout each stage of the product development process. In other words, we can clearly trace customer requirements from the start of product planning down to the most detailed instructions at the operating level. This necessitates that the ends and means are linked at each stage—that we have a system.

The voice of the customer is the point of departure for QFD and drives the process. Listening, understanding, interpreting, and translating what the customer says form the philosophical heart of QFD. It is important that QFD team members share a common understanding and knowledge of a product's objectives based on this expanded product definition step. Extraordinary efforts to collect and understand the unsolicited comments of potential and current customers are a hallmark of successful Japanese applications of QFD.

THE STRUCTURE OF QFD

QFD starts with a positive statement of what the customer wants and needs. In other words, What are the product objectives or the ends to which we are working? These are often referred to in QFD as the "whats." These are not necessarily product specifications, but may be more general in nature. For example, a commercial printer may tell the paper supplier that the paper must not tear while it is running on a rotary press.

However, we know that we cannot act specifically or directly on such general requirements. Therefore, we must specify, in our own internal technical language, what means we will use to accomplish our ends. At the product planning stage, these are often called substitute characteristics or design requirements. More generally, in QFD we call them the "hows." So, for our example, we might translate the customer's requirement of no paper tears into design requirements for thickness, width, and tensile strength. We should also determine objective target values that are as specific as possible. Width and thickness might then be assigned targets measured in millimeters, and tensile strength might be assigned targets measured in pounds of force.

Except for the simplest of products, the relationships between the "whats" and "hows" can quickly become confusing. One way to solve this problem is to form a matrix from the lists of "whats" and "hows" and to show the relationship between them using various symbols. Figure 2 is a simplified version of this most basic QFD tool.

The matrix is, of course, a simple concept, but it is a disciplined way to compare two sets of items. It provides a logical, in-depth look at many critical aspects of product or service. In short, it helps to ensure that things do not fall through the cracks.

Although this matrix represents the basic logic of all QFD charts, many options and enhancements are commonly used. For example, important weighting systems are frequently used and can help systematically and successively apply the Pareto principle, that is, elaborate the details at one stage, then select the most important items for the next stage. Thus, QFD can tell where to concentrate the engineering effort and, just as importantly, where not to invest time and money.

Another option for product planning is to make competitive evaluations of the "whats" and "hows":

FIGURE 2
Simplified Relationship Matrix

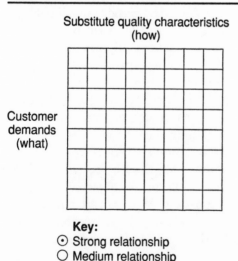

Key:
⊙ Strong relationship
○ Medium relationship
△ Weak relationship

- Ask customers how well you fare against the competition in terms of their most important requirements.
- Ask your engineers how you rate against the competition in terms of the technical requirements specified for the product.

Together, these evaluations can often pinpoint how to gain a competitive advantage and where improvement may be needed most.

A correlation matrix, in which the "hows" are compared against each other, can also identify conflicting design requirements. For example, the design requirements for a diesel engine may include targets for acceleration and particulate emissions. These two requirements might have a strong negative correlation in the sense that as the emissions improve, the acceleration worsens. This type of exercise helps detect possible trade-offs early on—a primary goal of QFD.

Figure 3 shows a conceptual product planning matrix that includes all enhancements previously described. Often referred to as the "House of Quality," it is almost always the first chart to be completed in a QFD study.

This matrix identifies a handful of key customer requirements and substitute characteristics that will become the focus of the rest of the QFD study. In general, these characteristics are transferred onto subsequent charts to be explored in more detail. Figure 4 is a simplified example of a completed House of Quality for the paper roll example.

The number of phases (or translations) needed to move from general customer requirements to highly specific production process controls varies with the product's complexity. As with much of QFD, there are no absolute rules—use as much or as little as necessary to ensure that key customer requirements will be met every time. In this regard, there are two general rules:

- Use what makes sense to you.
- Do not make things foreign to people.

Many managers think of QFD in somewhat discrete phases. The phases for an assembled product are generally described in

FIGURE 3
Conceptual Product Planning Matrix

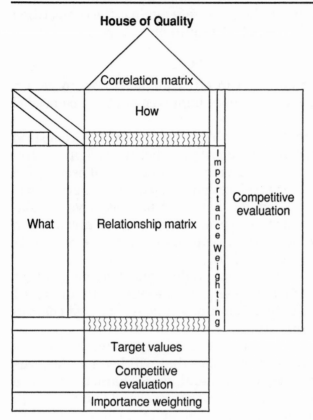

a fashion similar to the scheme shown in Figure 5 (although many more charts than what is shown might be involved in phases two, three, and four).

This process seems rather complicated, but the potential rewards are great. Many U.S. companies are becoming convinced that the rewards are worth the extra upfront effort in planning, execution, and top management involvement. Toyota and NGK, for example, report that their design cycle has been reduced by one third. Toyota further reports that start-up costs on one product line were reduced by 61 percent over a seven-year period that covered four start-ups. Aisin Warner claims

FIGURE 4
House of Quality

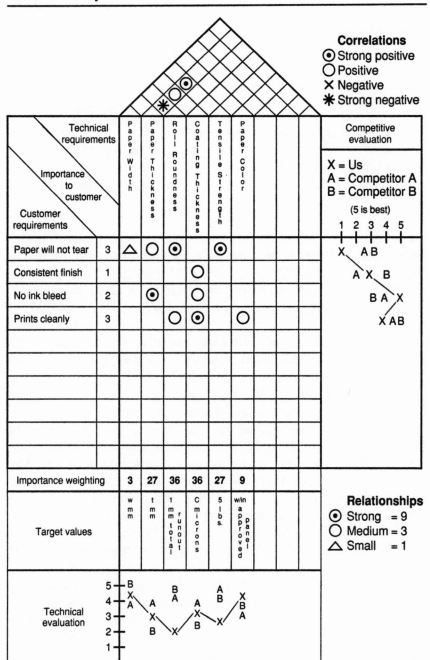

FIGURE 5
Discrete Phases of an Assembled Product's Process

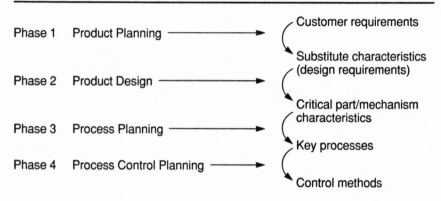

that the number of engineering changes and their design cycles have been halved. Komatsu MEC, a manufacturer of heavy equipment, used QFD to introduce 11 new products within a two-and-a-half-year development cycle, five of them simultaneously. These products earned a high degree of gains in market share.

QFD has also been applied successfully to mature products. For example, the Tokyo Juki Kogyo Co. used QFD to help direct the redesign of its line of sewing machines. It began by taking extraordinary measures to collect and comprehend information from the market, including detailed observations and discussions with machine operators and evaluation of complaint reports. One key customer demand was the ease with which cloth could be handled at the start of a sewing operation. The company's technical analysis and customer survey of competitors' machines further revealed that improvement in this area would provide a significant competitive advantage. The QFD process guided it to target key design characteristics, such as bed cross section and holding height, for intensive engineering effort.

The result of this effort was that the machines materially improved customers' quality and productivity. Kogyo sales increased despite a long-term decline in the sewing machine market.

Although many Japanese companies are using QFD, including all Toyota suppliers, the first U.S. case studies did not emerge until early 1986. However, interest is very great. All of the Big Three domestic automakers have begun QFD training and applications. Ford is strongly encouraging the use of QFD by its suppliers. Other automotive suppliers have already completed case studies and are using QFD on an ongoing basis. Nonautomotive users include such diverse companies as Omark Industries, Digital Equipment Corp., and Procter & Gamble.

QFD applications in the United States have so far been generally more modest in scope and impact than in Japan. Nevertheless, success stories are already emerging. For example, the QFD coordinator for an automotive supplier reported that a QFD team uncovered a problem with a glove compartment design that would likely have gone undetected for another year.

TIE-IN TO TAGUCHI

One of the reasons that QFD is so powerful is that it helps determine and rank critical items to which quality technology and engineering effort should be applied. In addition, QFD will often identify conflicting design requirements. In these instances, the use of experimental design methods, including the Taguchi methods, can provide some remarkable results. In fact, some Japanese companies attribute the majority of their total improvement in quality over the last 10 years to the use of designed experiments. However, they also give credit to the use of QFD as a planning mechanism that helps them get the biggest bang for the buck. Those serious about QFD should learn more about experimental design and other tools commonly used with QFD, such as fault tree analysis (FTA), failure mode and effect analysis (FMEA), and other general planning tools. The remainder of this chapter is an overview of the use and benefits of Taguchi methods.

While Taguchi methods are often an integral part of QFD, they are also used extensively outside of the QFD framework. For instance, fewer than 100 QFD case studies have been mented in the United States, but there have been over 6,000 Taguchi applications, and that number is growing rapidly. Dr. Genichi Taguchi, a highly acclaimed Japanese engineer and the winner of four Deming prizes, began developing these methods in Japan during the 1950s. His most important contribution has been the combination of engineering and statistical methods to achieve rapid improvements in cost and quality, accomplished through product and process design optimization. Taguchi's methods form a quality engineering system, which includes a number of special techniques. However, for the purpose of this discussion, we can distill the Taguchi approach to quality into the three following areas:

- How to evaluate quality.
- How to improve quality cost effectively.
- How to maintain quality cost effectively.

Taguchi defines and evaluates quality via his "loss function." Loss here refers to costs incurred or profits forgone relative to some baseline of performance. The underlying principle is that quality loss, measured in monetary units, is a function of the deviation from a target value (or ideal performance level) over the life of a product. Therefore, conformance to arbitrary specification limits is an irrelevant measure of quality (see Figure 6). The loss function provides a way to quantify the potential savings that can be achieved by reducing variation around the target value. This is in contrast to the notion that everything within specs is equally good and that everything outside of specs is equally bad. A simple illustration of this principle is variation occurring around a scheduled flight departure time. Customer dissatisfaction (and potential loss) will grow at an increasing rate as departure time deviates, early or late, from the published schedule. We can assign no arbitrary limits to distinguish zones of total satisfaction (no loss) from total dissatisfaction. Assume our standard on the "late" side is "no greater than 30 minutes." A delayed passenger certainly sees no black-and-white difference between a delay of 29.5 minutes and 30.5 minutes, and, therefore, our spec is a useless measure of quality.

FIGURE 6
Continuous Loss Function

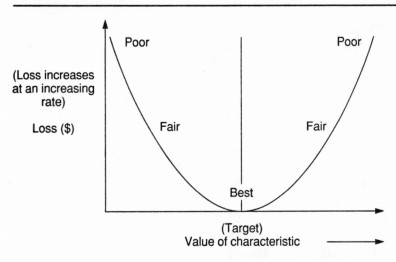

As a product example, consider the color density of a picture tube. It is unreasonable to assume that customers are equally satisfied with all density levels within a given specification interval, only to become totally dissatisfied when the density reaches certain discrete points. Suppose that two plants producing the same picture tube shipped units with the same average density, all within specifications. Both plants' customers should be equally satisfied, right? The Sony Corporation found out differently when customer satisfaction was higher and warranty claims lower for units produced in its Japanese plant than those produced in its American plant. The difference was in the deviation from the target value. While average density was the same, there was much greater dispersion in density values for the units produced in the United States.

The preceding are examples of cases where "nominal is best." The loss function also applies to "larger is better" situations (e.g., tread life, weld strength) and to "smaller is better" (e.g., fuel consumption, CO content of exhaust gas).

Using the loss function, all quality improvements are measured in terms of cost savings. Cost and quality improvement become one and the same. Quality projects may sometimes be undertaken even though no out-of-spec material is being produced. Conversely, it is possible that you will reject an improvement project in favor of others, even when some out-of-spec material is being produced. This view of quality greatly promotes the incessant devotion to reducing variation and to continuous improvement. This devotion accounts in large measure for Japan's rise as a global quality *and* cost leader.

The "how to" of improvement consists of three steps applied to both the product and the production processes:

1. *System design*—a nonstatistical process of surveying and selecting the appropriate design technology and concepts to produce a prototype design possessing the functions required by the product plan.

2. *Parameter design*—experimental design methods to find the optimal level of the individual system parameters, which were determined during the system design.

3. *Tolerance design*—experimental design methods used only after parameter design to set the tolerance of the parameters, if necessary. According to Taguchi, "Narrow tolerances should be the weapon of last resort to be used only when parameter design gives insufficient results."

Taguchi refers to these collectively as "off-line quality control." Of Taguchi's three steps, U.S. companies have applied parameter design the most extensively. The premise behind parameter design is strikingly simple. It is much easier and less costly to design a product insensitive to manufacturing variables than it is to control all of those variables. Similarly, it can be used to improve a product's field performance so that it is less subject to environmental variables and to deterioration. The object is to produce what is termed a "robust" design.

As an example, Taguchi often cites the case of the Ina Tile Company (1953). Ina knew that uneven temperature distribution in the tunnel kiln was an assignable cause of size variation in the fired tiles. Rather than attempting to control the kiln temperature, which would have been expensive, a designed experiment was performed. The experiment studied the effects of varying seven features of the tile mixture. They found that by changing the lime content from 1 to 5 percent, tile size variation was reduced by a factor of ten, obviating the need for expensive temperature controls.

In parameter design, Taguchi uses a modification of the conventional statistical methods of experimental design. The basic strategy is straightforward:

- Identify which factors are controllable and which are "noise" (not controllable or expensive to control).
- Find the levels for controllable factors so that highest performance is achieved despite the noise.

The power of the Taguchi methods lies in their ability to arrive at a greatly improved design or production process in a short time period, using only a relatively small number of experiments. To check for the effects of only four factors, each at three different settings, you must contend with 81 combinations when using the classical design techniques. A corresponding Taguchi experiment would use only nine combinations to check for the factors' effects. This difference grows exponentially as more factors are added to the analysis. As a check on the initial experimental conclusions using Taguchi methods, a small number of confirmatory experiments are usually performed.

Companies have frequently applied the Taguchi strategy to the controllable factors in an existing production process, without modification to the product design itself. The Ford Body and Assembly Division used the Taguchi approach to improve door fits under existing production constraints in one of its plants. They had only four factors to use (e.g., latch plate location), yet they managed to improve on three of five targeted quality characteristics, without capital investment or design changes. ITT used Taguchi methods to increase the weld-splice strength in wire harness assemblies to the point where it exceeded the core strength of the wire. Not only did they save $300,000 per year by discontinuing a destructive pull test, they also reduced field failures and eliminated the need to invest in costly alternative processes, such as ultrasonic welding.

Even if the product and process could be completely optimized, sources of product variation remain—tools still wear out, people still make mistakes, and materials still vary. To maintain quality *during* production, Taguchi has developed what he calls "on-line quality control." This relies on several mathematical formulas to cost effectively minimize losses due to piece-to-piece variation. These losses are due to scrap, adjustment, inspection, and manufacturing-related performance variation. The basic principle is to weigh the cost (loss) of reducing variation around the target against the loss due to the variation itself. This form of quality control does not involve any charts, but rather, it requires a systematic method of checking and adjusting. Currently, on-line quality control is neither practiced nor well understood in the United States, even though it is well suited to certain operations, such as metal stamping.

PERSPECTIVES ON TAGUCHI

Of course, Taguchi is not without his critics. Some charge that his methods lack statistical "sophistication," that they are statistically incorrect and inefficient, and sometimes that they give the incorrect, i.e., not "the best" answer. The argument may really represent the difference between a 50 percent improvement in two months versus a 90 percent improvement in two years. In reality, with a complex product or process, the full conventional experimental protocol is almost never performed and seat-of-the-pants judgments are often left to suffice.

Perhaps more important than Taguchi's statistical methods is the conceptual framework for quality improvement he has provided. While the critics' arguments against his statistical procedures have merit and should be addressed, what Taguchi has done is to make statistical techniques accessible and usable to a wide range of nonstatisticians. Unlike conventional statistical techniques, which have been used to advantage in relatively isolated instances, Taguchi's methods actually have had a great impact on American products and the way in which manufacturing companies operate. Perhaps this impact can best be measured by the many documented cases of significant cost savings and the overwhelmingly enthusiastic response to Taguchi. ITT, for example, has used Taguchi methods in over 2,000 cases with reported cost savings of $35 million. Many other cases of six- even seven-figure cost savings abound in the literature, and the interest here is growing. A recent two-day conference in the Detroit area on Taguchi methods and QFD drew a full house of 250 people, with many more turned away.

More telling, perhaps, is Mr. Akashi Fukuhara's analysis of quality improvement sources at Toyota from 1977 to 1985. Mr. Fukuhara is vice-president of the Central Japan Quality Association and the retired manager of product assurance at Toyota Autobody. He attributes fully 50 percent of improvements to Taguchi's parameter design and the remainder to the use of fault tree analysis (FTA) and failure mode and effect analysis (FMEA). He believes that many other Japanese firms would give a similar breakdown. These firms still generally use SPC to monitor and to maintain the quality improvements made in the design stages, as well as the reduction in variation they have achieved through the application of SPC over many years.

SUMMARY

SPC should be an important element of a company's goal to achieve world-class quality and productivity. However, the responsibility for quality must be extended to all functions of the business. Quality efforts should begin at the very inception of a product, using the voice of the customer as a constant guide. The timing and relationships among QFD, Taguchi methods, and other operating principles of "world-class' companies are depicted in Figure 7. QFD is an appropriate mechanism to integrate these principles and methods, where the voice of the customer selectively guides the application of efforts to eliminate waste and to foster continuous improvement.

Every organization already has some means of eventually incorporating customers' presumed requirements into a final product. In this sense, QFD certainly does not represent a totally new or radical idea. However, through QFD, companies do this in a very disciplined, structured, and methodical manner, most often through the use of a series of charts or matrices, as a means to achieve specific product objectives and to translate customer requirements into requirements that people within the organization can understand and act on.

FIGURE 7
Relationships among QFD, Taguchi Methods, and JIT/TQC Operating Principles

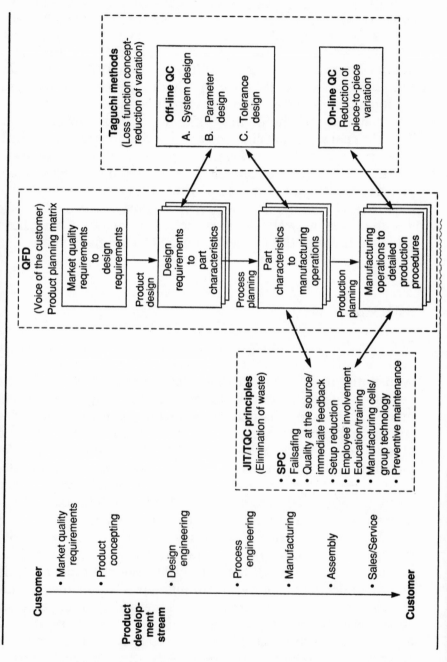

Given that the main objective of any company is to preempt the competition by bringing products to market sooner, with improved quality, at a lower cost, and with greater customer acceptance, those companies that embrace QFD and the use of Taguchi methods may well be distinguished as the leaders in the worldwide battle for market share.

CHAPTER 9

QUALITY OF CONFORMANCE TO DESIGN

Ernest C. Huge

Quality of conformance to design is the degree to which the product or service conforms to the intended design requirements. Quality of manufacturing is another phrase used by some manufacturing companies to identify the same concept.

The relationship between design and conformance quality can be illustrated with a comparison of a fast-food restaurant with a gourmet restaurant. McDonald's restaurants have obviously been designed to satisfy a different set of customer needs than those satisfied by five-star gourmet restaurants, as summarized in the following.

Quality Characteristics	McDonald's	Five-Star Gourmet Restaurant
Variety	Limited	Broad
Convenience	Very important	Unimportant
Price	Low	High
Atmosphere	Little	Great
Speed of service	Fast	Unrushed
Individualized attention	Very little	Great

It cannot really be said that the quality of the gourmet restaurant's design is better than McDonald's because it costs more, only that it is different. Many people incorrectly relate higher quality in every respect (including conformance to design) with higher prices. Although the prices of meals offered at McDonald's are only one thirtieth to one fortieth of the gourmet restaurant's prices, the conformance quality at McDonald's is much better than many gourmet restaurants. In fact, McDonald's has become synonymous with consistency. Customers receive the same-tasting food and the same service almost everywhere. By having a good design and a quality that conforms to its design better than other fast-food providers, McDonald's has a significant competitive advantage that is reflected in its leading market share.

On the other hand, having perfect conformance quality will not ensure success. Quality, as perceived by customers, can only be as good as the intent of the design. There is no way for conformance quality to make up for a bad design. Even with excellent conformance quality McDonald's design must be right or nearly right for the fast-food market. This chapter:

• Builds upon the prior chapter, which initiated a discussion of the integration of conformance and design quality, by comparing the various approaches to ensuring quality of conformance to design.
• Recommends how and when to best utilize the various approaches, especially statistical process control (SPC). Many large companies have mandated that their suppliers use SPC.

APPROACHES TO ENSURING QUALITY OF CONFORMANCE TO DESIGN

The traditional approach to ensuring quality of conformance to design has been to detect defects by conducting inspections at various stages of the production process, frequently by taking samples of various lots. By sorting good from bad, inspection helps to ensure that the final product shipped to the customer is correct. However, it does not improve quality. Further, as Figure 1 shows, even though the sample passes, there is a fairly good chance that bad parts will get through.

FIGURE 1
Sample Inspection

Probability that No Defects Will Be Found in Sample of 10 Pieces	
True Defect Rate (%)	Probability None Found
20	11/100
10	35/100
5	60/100
1*	90/100
0.27	97/100

*For 1 percent defect rate: none found 9 out of 10 times. 1% ≈ 4 times higher rate than OEMs permit.

In short, as a means to ensure quality, inspection does not work well and is costly. Most companies that depend upon inspection for quality control will not survive in the 1990s.

PARADIGM SHIFT FROM DETECTION TO PREVENTION

For a company to be successful, quality must be ensured by controlling the processes that result in the desired product or service. Controlling processes prevents defects. Improving processes improves quality.

Controlling and improving a process are synonomous with controlling and reducing process variation, which were discussed in Chapters 1 and 5. As explained previously, there are essentially two causes of variation—common causes and special or assignable causes. Variation due to common causes occurs continually in every process and is predictable because it follows a stable distribution or pattern over a period of time. For example, a scale was used to weigh the same material 100 times. A plot of these individual weighings resulted in the normal distribution shown in Figure 2.

Subsequent weighings will fall randomly somewhere within this distribution. The exact cause of variation from one weigh-

FIGURE 2

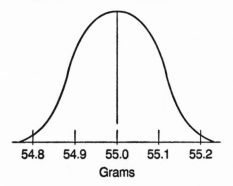

ing to another cannot be identified. In general, however, the variation can be attributed to the ever present common causes of variation in the mechanism of the scale and in the weighing process.

In addition to common causes, variation can be due to specific, identifiable causes. For example, a substitute chemical process operator was inadequately trained and did not follow the correct procedure for changing equipment. As a result, the material was contaminated and had to be discarded. This type of variation—due to special causes—does not occur randomly and is not predictable.

PROCESS CAPABILITY

When a process exhibits variation due only to common causes, it is said to be stable or in a state of statistical control. However, statistical control may not be good enough to meet customer needs, as shown in Figure 3. Even though the process is perfectly centered within the specification limits (i.e., the process mean is the target value), a certain percentage of the time the process will be outside the specification limits. In these cases, the process is incapable: it cannot meet specifications. For example, a weighing process having a capability of ±0.1 milligram cannot meet a ±0.01 milligram requirement.

FIGURE 3

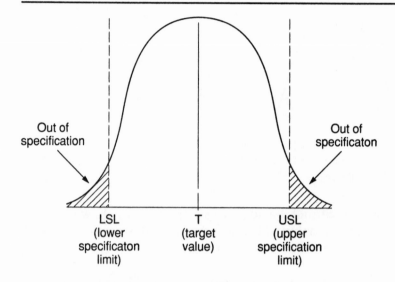

Out of specification

Out of specificaton

LSL
(lower
specificaton
limit)

T
(target
value)

USL
(upper
specification
limit)

In Figure 4 the process average has shifted significantly away from the target value, although the spread of the process remained the same. Consequently, much more of the output is outside of the specifications.

In Figure 5, requirements are met 100 percent of the time, even though the process is not centered on the target value. This perfect outcome results because the inherent variability is small.

FIGURE 4
After Process Shift

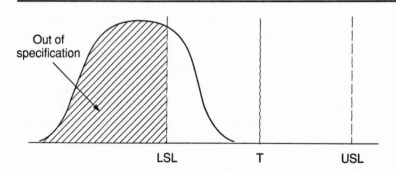

Out of specification

LSL   T   USL

FIGURE 5

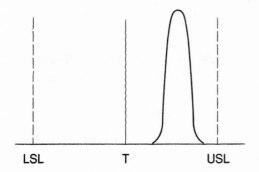

LSL   T   USL

Thus, conformance to the design requirements depends upon both the process capability and the degree to which the process is centered on target.

The capability index (Cpk) indicates the relationship between the process capability and the design specifications. Cpk can only be calculated after stability has been achieved. As an example, assume that the process is in control and has a normal distribution, as shown in Figure 6.

In Figure 6, s stands for standard deviation, which is a measure of the spread or range of the distribution from the mean. Plus/minus 3s includes 99.73 percent of the total distribution.

FIGURE 6

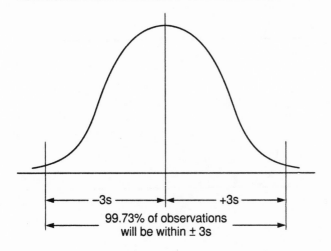

-3s ———————— +3s ————

99.73% of observations
will be within ± 3s

Cpk is defined as

$$\frac{USL - \bar{X}}{3s} \quad \text{or} \quad \frac{\bar{X} - LSL}{3s} \quad \text{whichever is less}$$

For example, if the situation shown in Figure 7 exists, where USL = 8.0, LSL = 0.0, $\bar{X}$ = 2.0, and s = 0.5, then

$$\frac{8-2}{1.5} = 4 \qquad \frac{2-0}{1.5} = 1.33$$

Therefore, Cpk = 1.33, the lesser value. A Cpk of 1.33 is considered the minimum for process capability.

Dr. Genichi Taguchi has developed a method for economically evaluating how capable a process should be. Taguchi's loss function expresses the degree to which the design is not satisfied (i.e., what he calls loss to society) in terms of the difference between the target value and the process average $(T - \bar{X})$ and the variability of the process (V^2), as shown in the following.

$$L = C\,[(T-X) + V^2]$$

where C = cost constant, T = target value for a given quality characteristic, X = process average, and V^2 = process variation (with a normal distribution V^2 equals 6s).

The loss function is a way to show the economic value of reducing variation and staying closer to target. Engineering's job, which Taguchi calls off-line quality engineering, is to establish

FIGURE 7

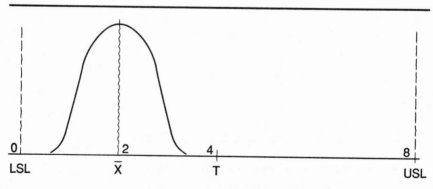

the design target for the least cost and to reduce process variation by adroit process design. Manufacturing's job, which Taguchi calls on-line quality engineering, is to keep the process average as close to the target as possible. The loss function also shows that manufacturing alone cannot ensure quality of conformance to design. For this reason, calling quality of conformance to design "quality of manufacturing" is erroneous.

WHY IT IS IMPORTANT TO KNOW THE NATURE OF THE CAUSE OF VARIATION

Knowing the nature of the cause of variation is important because the strategies for dealing with variation due to common causes are different than for variation due to special causes.

With special causes the following must be provided:

- Immediate feedback that there is a problem.
- Immediate reaction to the feedback.
- Problem identification and solution.

Corrective action for variation due to special causes can usually be accomplished without the intervention of management and is frequently short term. A fundamental process change is not required. Eliminating a special cause does not improve the process (i.e., the capability of the process). If a production process is running and there is evidence of a special cause, then the special cause should be investigated and fixed, even though the parts produced still satisfy customer requirements.

As stated previously, even when special causes have been eliminated, the process capability may not be good enough to satisfy customer requirements. If not, then a fundamental process change is required. Process changes such as these usually require a longer term solution and management's attention since processes usually cannot be improved by people who work in that process.

Sometimes it is difficult to immediately determine whether variation is due to common causes or to special causes. For example, the errors made by 50 distributors in processing shipping orders averaged two per month and exhibited stability. This indicates a system of common causes. However, during one month, shipping had to correct 100 errors. The sales manager's initial reaction was to send a scathing letter to all distributors and to add an instructional session to the agenda of the next distributors' meeting. Closer scrutiny, however, showed that all but two errors were made by five distributors. Further analysis revealed these special causes:

- Three distributors had old price sheets.
- Two distributors were new and needed individual training.

On the other hand, all distributors make occasional errors. This suggests a common cause system; that is, errors are due to the inherent capability of the system. Reducing the error rate would, therefore, require a fundamental system change, such as redesigning the order form and/or providing training for all distributors.

HOW DO YOU KNOW WHETHER VARIATION IS DUE TO SPECIAL CAUSES OR TO COMMON CAUSES?

Statistical process control (SPC), developed by Walter Shewhart of AT&T in the 1930s, provides a quantitative way to determine if variation is due to common causes or to special causes. SPC uses control charts based on statistical laws. These laws show that variation averages of samples follow a normal distribution. Control limits are set at ±3s (see Figure 8).

Recall that ±3s includes 99.73 percent of the distribution. Since there is a 99.73 percent probability that any given point will fall within the control limits, the probability of a point falling outside the limits is so low that if it does happen, it can be concluded that this is due to special causes. Furthermore, even though points fall within the control limits, there can be evidence of special causes because the pattern suggests nonran-

FIGURE 8
Components of a Control Chart

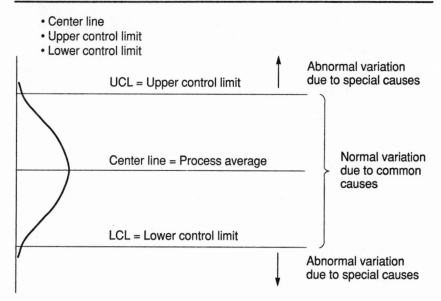

- Center line
- Upper control limit
- Lower control limit

UCL = Upper control limit

Abnormal variation
due to special causes

Center line = Process average

Normal variation
due to common
causes

LCL = Lower control limit

Abnormal variation
due to special causes

domness (i.e., the pattern would not appear if each point occurred randomly). Examples of control charts showing evidence of special causes are provided in Figure 9.

Run charts, which simply plot data over time, can also be used to determine whether or not there is evidence of special causes. Although run charts are easier to use because they require fewer calculations, they are less sensitive than average and range charts. Refer to the appendix for run chart rules.

Having a stable system where no variation is due to special causes is not a natural occurrence. When analyzing processes initially, almost all are unstable. Once a process is stabilized, effort is required to maintain that stability. Improving the process capability requires even more energy. The graphic and accompanying explanation shown in Figure 10 were developed by the Gleason Components Group, a division of the Gleason Corporation. It has become the logo of their continuous improvement process and is used by permission of their dynamic and visionary president, Don Sweet.

FIGURE 9

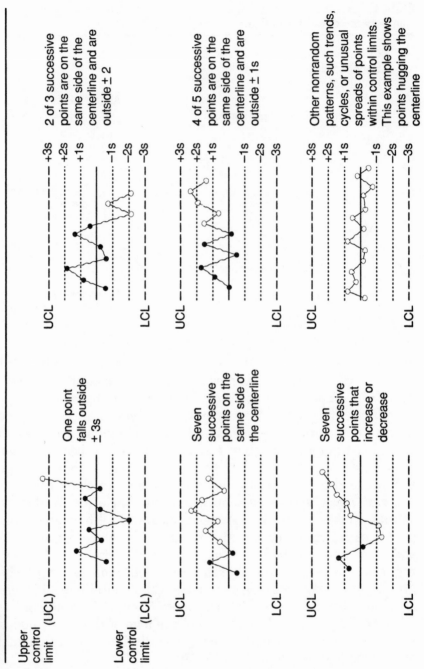

FIGURE 10

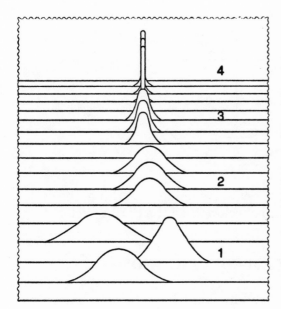

The stages of continuous improvement include the following:

1. Instability. Includes both off-target and inconsistent variability. This is usually present in everything (due to assignable causes) when it is statistically analyzed for the first time.

2. Stability. Eliminating special causes of variation results in stable output. This creates predictable and reliable performance in the future. However, this output is still off target.

3. Targeting. The variability is now centered on the target. The remaining variability is due to system/ common causes of variation.

4. Continuous reduction of variability around the target. This is indicated by the narrowing distribution curves, which further reduce the system/common causes of variation. This process continues ad infinitum.

IMPROVING THE PROCESS

The generic approach used for all process improvement is summarized by the Shewhart cycle shown in Figure 11. The approach starts with planning and moves counterclockwise through the cycle.

The Shewhart cycle is also known as the plan-do-check-act cycle, or simply the PDCA cycle. It really amounts to the application of the scientific method to process improvement.

FIGURE 11

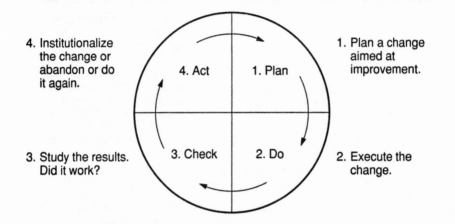

When applied to improve a method of doing something, the cycle is known as standardize-do-check-act, or the SDCA cycle.

BASIC SEVEN PROBLEM-SOLVING TOOLS

Many problems can be solved by what have become known as the "basic seven" problem-solving tools. These tools are the Pareto analysis, the process flow chart, the check sheet, the cause-and-effect diagram, the histogram, the scatter diagram, and the control chart.

1. *Pareto analysis* applies the 80/20 rule to identify the significant few causes that account for most of the problem. It separates the "vital few" from the "trivial many." All potential causes or variation problems are ranked according to their contribution to cost, variation, or other measure (see Figure 12).

2. *Process flow chart* depicts the relevant steps in a process and aids understanding of a process (see Figure 13).

3. *Check sheet* provides quantitative evidence of the frequency of events. For example, it can be used to verify that what people *feel* is a problem really is a problem (see Figure 14).

4. *Cause-and-effect diagram* depicts and organizes by major category the potential causes of the undesired or desired effect (see Figure 15).

FIGURE 12
Causes of Machine Breakdown

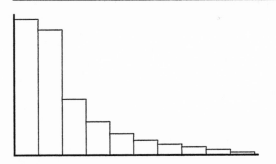

FIGURE 13

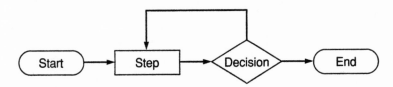

FIGURE 14

		Day				
Problem	1	2	3	4	5	Total
A	II	IIII	I	II	NN	14
B	I	II	I		II	6
C	IIII	III	I	III	NN	16
D	II	II	III	I	II	10
Total	9	11	6	6	14	46

5. *Histogram* displays the distribution of the number real variables, such as weight, in frequency form. This is a way to evaluate the data visually (see Figure 16).

6. *Scatter diagram* helps to study the relationship between data (see Figure 17).

7. *Control chart* (Figure 18) is used to determine the nature of the cause of variation (i.e., common causes or special causes).

FIGURE 15

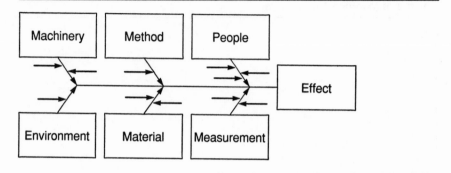

FIGURE 16

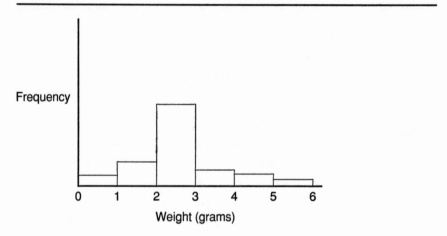

FIGURE 17

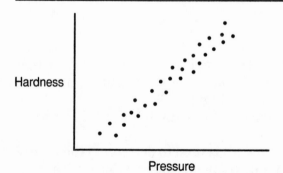

FIGURE 18

_ _ _ <u>Upper control limit</u> _ _ _ _

Average

_ _ _ <u>Lower control limit</u> _ _ _ _

Time

When using these tools, an improvement team first identifies a problem. For example, in one company the problem was order acceptance errors. A control chart of errors showed that the process was out of control (i.e., there was evidence of special cause). The team had already flowcharted the order acceptance process to gain a better understanding of it. By brainstorming, the team identified possible root causes, which were organized using the cause-and-effect diagram. When a potential root cause was identified, the team asked why five times to ensure that the true root cause was identified. Asking why five times revealed the information shown in Figure 19.

FIGURE 19
Potential Root Cause

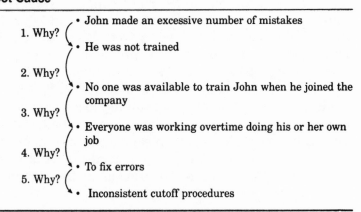

1. Why?
- John made an excessive number of mistakes
- He was not trained

2. Why?
- No one was available to train John when he joined the company

3. Why?
- Everyone was working overtime doing his or her own job

4. Why?
- To fix errors

5. Why?
- Inconsistent cutoff procedures

The team next identified potential root causes, limiting this list to the significant few. A check sheet was developed to collect data to verify the significant few root causes. By applying the 80/20 rule, or Pareto analysis, the team determined that an inconsistent data processing cutoff accounted for at least 90% of the problems. Consequently, the team redesigned a fail-safe cutoff procedure to ensure consistency and then implemented the change. Subsequent checking showed that implementing this change all but eliminated order acceptance errors. The team then completed the last phase of the Shewhart cycle: they took steps to institutionalize the change. Furthermore, John was trained by a competent trainer.

When getting started with improvement teams, these seven basic tools can be used to solve many problems. However, in most manufacturing companies, world-class quality also requires much more powerful techniques, such as design of experiments.

SPC OVERKILL

Many large O.E.M. companies have mandated that their suppliers implement SPC, which essentially means that these suppliers must methodically use the basic seven tools, *especially control charts*. Responding to customer demands, many suppliers have generated control charts on the shop floor as evidence of their commitment to SPC. However, in many of those companies, there are too many charts and too little problem solving. In many traditional manufacturing companies applying control charts on the shop floor is somewhat analogous to using a surgeon's scalpel to cut down a tree. Many companies need to first solve the obvious, chronic problems that employees have been telling them about for years (e.g., overhaul worn-out equipment, organize and clean up the shop floor). Widespread application of simple problem-solving tools, such as flowcharts, Pareto analysis, check sheets, and cause-and-effect diagrams will solve a lot of problems. When companies first apply the quality improvement process, the many special causes are usually very well known by the people operating in the system; a control chart is not needed to distinguish between common causes and special causes of variation. The employees can "cherry pick" those problems. Consequently, after all the cherries are picked, the special causes are not spotted as easily, and the company's quality improvement levels off. At this point, statistical process control is needed to differentiate between the special causes and the common causes and to maintain continuous improvement.

Everyone, especially management, needs to understand why it is important to know the nature of the causes of variation. The underlying theory of SPC is the basis for much of what represents "new quality paradigm thinking." However, world-class quality will not be obtained and sustained by applying control charts alone.

When touring world-class Japanese companies, many visitors are surprised that there are no visible control charts. These companies have improved many of their processes to such a degree (i.e., Cpk's that range from 2 to 30) that maintaining control charts is unnecessary.

Additionally, control charts are still after the fact. The process still needs to run first in order to generate the data analyzed by a control chart. Consequently, these charts are not the ultimate prevention tool. The ultimate solution is to design a process that can be operated only in the correct way. One way to do this is to fail-safe the process. The Japanese call fail-safing "pokayoke." Examples of fail-safing include the following:

1. Designing parts that can be assembled only the correct way.

2. Design of a storage device that can store only the correct number of parts, thereby eliminating miscounts. One example of this is a pegboard used to store gaskets. A colored mark on the peg corresponds to the correct number stored, as shown in Figure 20.

3. To prevent the omission of a spring or screw during assembly, one electronics company now requires the assembler to put two screws and two springs into a dish at the beginning of each assembly. After completing the assembly, the assembler looks into the dish to ensure that the screws and springs are not there.

FIGURE 20

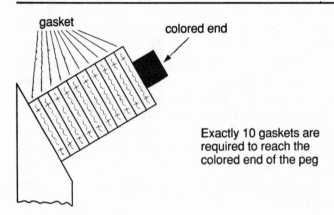

gasket

colored end

Exactly 10 gaskets are
required to reach the
colored end of the peg

4. A retailer's old policy was to send only invoices to customers. However, every month a number of payments were late because errors were made when customers addressed envelopes or the envelopes were mailed without stamps. To eliminate these problems, the retailer now includes a self-addressed stamped envelope with the invoice.

Unfortunately, not all processes lend themselves to failsafing. The next-best process design immediately detects problems at the problem source at a very low cost. This really amounts to 100 percent inspection of all items. For example, after filling a box with Christmas ornaments, the operator pushes a button to move the box to shipping. The button activates a scale, which weighs the box and contents. If the weight is incorrect, another light goes on to tell the operator that the box is not full. Toyota coined the word "autonomation" for such a process; this stops when there is a quality problem. Corrective action, however, still requires manual intervention.

It is possible though, for corrective action to be totally automated. One type of computerized bending machine does this. It detects variation in raw material and adjusts the process parameters, such as pressure and bend angle, automatically.

A great many processes are quite complex, having a large number of critical process characteristics. In these cases, design of experiments (DOE) can be used to identify those characteristics that have the greatest effect on the process. Control efforts can then be focused toward the "critical few" to reduce the need to monitor a large number of parameters.

Despite the use of DOE to reduce variability and SPC to maintain process control, processes degrade over time unless effort is expanded to counteract this natural tendency. A management system known as total productive maintenance (TPM) ensures not only that a system is maintained at the current standard (i.e., process capability), but that it is improved. Regular preventive maintenance is an initial stage of the development of a TPM system. TPM also entails an ongoing operator certification process as operators enhance their ability to operate, set up, maintain, and improve the capability and reliability of various equipment. Chapter 10 explains why TPM is essential to becoming a world-class manufacturing company.

CHAPTER 10

TOTAL PRODUCTIVE MAINTENANCE

J. R. Rodriguez

Many American executives have heard of the Deming Prize for quality, but few are familiar with the PM (Plant Maintenance) Distinguished Plant Award established by the Japan Institute of Plant Maintenance to recognize excellence in maintenance activities within manufacturing plants. The award was established in the early 1960s, just as the Japanese began to apply preventive and corrective maintenance know-how acquired during visits to the United States and Europe. By the 1970s application of the continuous learning process to maintenance techniques became known as total productive maintenance (TPM). In recent years, all PM Award winners have been TPM practitioners.

Figure 1 presents some results achieved by two PM Award winners resulting from their implementation of a TPM system. These improvements are even more impressive when one considers that they were realized after many years of continuous improvement activities based on the concepts of JIT and TQC. In fact, to realize fully the benefits of TPM, a company needs a strong JIT and TQC base.

TPM is a low-cost, people-intensive system for maximizing equipment effectiveness by involving all of a company's departments and functions in a preventive maintenance system. Its goal is not only to keep processes operational, but also to improve them. Ideally, a piece of equipment will perform better near the end of its life than when it was purchased.

As their investment in equipment and automation increased, Japanese companies discovered that they needed to emphasize equipment-oriented management techniques, such as TPM, in addition to JIT and TQC.

TPM utilizes many of the same process improvement techniques as JIT and TQC, but TPM relates them specifically to equipment management. Some of these techniques follow:

• Maintenance prevention, which is used to design virtually maintenance-free equipment.
• Life-cycle planning, which is used to predict the maintenance needs of equipment throughout its lifetime.
• MQM (man-quality-machine) management, which, in order to ensure defect-free products, analyzes the interface between maintenance, product quality, and machine parts and links

FIGURE 1
TPM Results: PM Prize Winners

Tangibles		
Company A		Company B
150% ↑	Labor productivity improvement	66% ↑
.01%	Current level of sudden breakdowns	.04%
25% ↓	Customer complaint reduction	25% ↓
Intangibles		
• Brought "*new life*" to "*used*" equipment		
• Closer coordination of sales, manufacturing, engineering		
• Problem solving based on facts		
• Greater confidence and pride		
• More knowledgeable work force		

specific maintenance procedures, machine actions, and machine parts to each product quality characteristic.

As with the JIT and TQC processes, the TPM process is driven by employee involvement at all company levels. TPM transfers primary responsibility for machine maintenance as close to the action as possible—to the machine operators. The goal of this responsibility transfer is to develop a highly coordinated approach to productive maintenance where everyone works together as part of the improvement process. Team activities are the catalyst for these changes. Operators are expected to maintain normal operating conditions, to engage in routine preventive maintenance, to inspect their machines daily, to routinely clean the equipment (which has the added benefit of encouraging a close examination of potential trouble spots), and to handle basic repairs. This frees the maintenance department of the time-consuming process of responding only to catastrophic problems. Maintenance employees can then perform more diagnostic and analytical work to counter potential problems and improve operations. These employees can also instruct machine operators in basic maintenance skills.

Another key component of TPM is education and training. To fulfill their new responsibilities, the operators need in-house instruction covering correct operating practices and simple repairs. This skills training can generally be provided by the maintenance department with minimal overhead.

Employee motivation, awareness, and recognition can be maintained through a licensing system requiring that only trained and qualified personnel perform maintenance on the equipment and through the "my machine" system, where the operator's name is put on the machine once he or she is qualified to maintain it. In the case of three-shift plants, the system is sometimes revised to "my inspection" to provide an opportunity for all three shifts to be involved.

A premise of the quality philosophy is that it is possible to attain zero defects by eliminating errors and preventing rejects. In TPM, achieving zero failures in machine operations is also considered possible. In fact, several PM Prize winners have achieved and maintained a state of operations where errors, defects, and failures are extremely rare.

THE FIVE PILLARS OF TPM

TPM is considered to have five pillars. These pillars follow:

- Productive maintenance.
- Proprietary technology.
- Quality maintenance.
- 5S.
- Training and education.

Productive Maintenance

Productive maintenance is one of the five TPM pillars. (see Figure 2). It comprises a system of preventive and corrective maintenance techniques. The objective of productive maintenance is to design equipment capable of attaining high operating times. Mean time between failures (MTBF), which ranks equipment by failure rates and analyzes the causes of those failures, is the key analysis tool. For example, MTBF might show that a problem is due to insufficient lubrication, thus indicating a need to improve lubrication schedules and systems.

To improve operating time, these factors, known as the "six big losses," must be reduced:

- Equipment failures.
- Set up and adjustments.
- Defectives.
- Yield losses.
- Minor stops.
- Reduced speed losses.

The key measure used with respect to these factors is equipment effectiveness and is calculated as follows:

$$\begin{aligned} \text{Equipment effectiveness} &= \text{Machine availability} \times \text{Performance efficiency} \times \text{Rate of quality} \\ &= \frac{\text{Planned time} - \text{downtime}}{\text{Planned time}} \times \frac{\text{Theoretical cycle time}}{\text{Actual cycle time}} \times \frac{\text{Good parts}}{\text{Parts produced}} \end{aligned}$$

FIGURE 2
The Key Supporting Elements of TPM

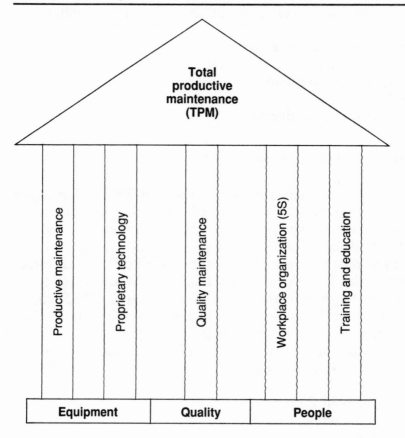

Theoretical cycle time assumes that set-up time is extremely short (i.e., less than or equal to 10 minutes). Actual cycle time includes run time and actual set-up time. By having such a short theoretical cycle time, this measurement is extremely rigorous.

Many of the recent winners of the PM Prize have equipment effectiveness ratios in excess of 85 percent. The ratios of the best plants in the United States on average are no higher than the low seventieth percentile. In average U.S. plants, this ratio ranges from 25 to 33 percent. It is important to point out that PM Prize winners must maintain this measurement of all equipment!

Basic maintenance activities performed by the operators themselves (i.e., lubrication, bolt tightening, cleaning tests, and measurements of vibration, heat, gauges) require extensive training. A licensing system ensures that these are performed by qualified employees.

Proprietary Technology

Development of proprietary technology is another equipment-based TPM activity. Many Japanese and American companies can design and manufacture their own production equipment. This capability generally brings lower cost, specific purpose machines into operations. When the process of designing and manufacturing this equipment in-house necessitates heavy involvement from operations and maintenance personnel, the likelihood of obtaining equipment liked by everyone is greatly increased. Other factors to be considered during this process include:

- Extent of automation.
- Degree of maintenance-free operation.
- Ease of start-up.
- Life-cycle costing.
- Energy usage.

Productive maintenance and the development of proprietary technology ensure feature-oriented effective production equipment, which provides competitive advantage because it cannot be purchased by competitors.

Quality Maintenance

Quality maintenance has two objectives: to build quality through equipment (ensure that no product defects are caused by faulty equipment) and to build a reliable production line (zero failures).

To achieve these objectives, TPM uses MTBF and MQM management to analyze parts, products, and maintenance actions, to verify the causes of problems, and to select proper countermeasures. MQM management also dissects operating mistakes to determine if additional training or fail-safing devices are appropriate countermeasures.

The operational standard of TPM quality management is simple:

	Accept		Failure
Do not	Manufacture	a	or
	Send		Defect

Workplace Organization: 5S

TPM organizes the workplace along five dimensions known as 5S for their original Japanese names: seiri—organization; seiton—orderliness; seiso—attention to details; seiketsu—cleanliness; and shitsuke—discipline. The 5S is designed to create a well-disciplined workplace by maintaining employee "awareness" of these key quality dimensions.

Visual management and qualification of operators (i.e., licensing) are two other important organizational techniques. A generic visual management PDCA cycle is shown in Figure 3. The focus is not on cleaning and housekeeping, but rather on

FIGURE 3
The Plan-Do-Check-Act Cycle of Workplace Organization

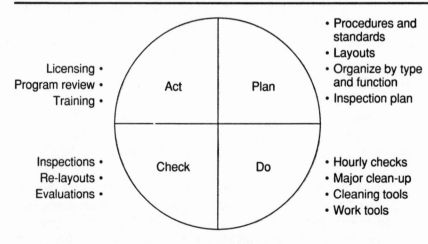

using the environment to provide information about and to prevent quality and productivity losses. The prevention aspect demands discipline, not in a punitive sense, but in the sense of a willingness to observe the rules.

The focal idea of 5S workplace organization is identifying all the subtle abnormalities that might cause failures or defects if not discovered and treated. Practicing 5S on a regular basis encourages the formation of an improvement cycle, beginning with reducing variations caused by abnormalities, then by creating stability and uniformity in the manufacturing processes, and finally by enhancing process analysis, which, in turn, leads to further improvements.

Because discovering abnormalities depends on being able to "touch" the equipment, "machine handkerchiefs" are used to keep the equipment clean. Such intimate involvement with the machine is likely to reveal any leaks, excessive vibration, loose bolts, etc. Identifying such problems early means that the problems can be corrected before a breakdown occurs and production is interrupted.

The purpose of the TPM licensing system referred to earlier is to expand an operator's capabilities by developing new skills and promoting operational stability. The system also encourages the acquisition of the skills necessary to perform multiple jobs, creating a multifunctional work force. There are two types of licenses: common and practical. A common (or general) license indicates plantwide skills (such as vibration measurement techniques), while the practical (or departmental) license covers maintenance skills specific to a department or type of machine. Operators wear badges indicating the licenses they have earned, and charts are posted in each department to showcase everyone's progress.

Training and Education

Within the TPM system, training and education efforts focus on disseminating maintenance and engineering know-how. The goal of these efforts is for each operator to be able to maintain his or her own equipment.

Engineering and maintenance personnel handle training, emphasizing practical knowledge about real machine part failures, often using three-dimensional models. The relationship between failures and improper operating procedures and poor maintenance is stressed.

Figure 4 lists the improvements that can be made using a TPM system. This listing is broken down by the five pillars of TPM.

CONCLUSION

In order to become world class, U.S. manufacturing companies need to dramatically change existing maintenance practices. As manufacturing grows increasingly more sophisticated and automated, trouble-free operation becomes imperative. TPM takes preventive maintenance practices beyond merely avoiding breakdowns to address the process capability issues crucial to producing defect-free products. It clearly demonstrates that equipment and maintenance improvements can be made with-

FIGURE 4
Objectives of TPM by Element

TPM element		Expected Improvements
Productive maintenance	⟶	Maximum equipment utilization
Quality maintenance	⟶	Build quality through equipment
Facility and equipment engineering	⟶	Development of proprietary technology
Workplace organization (5S)	⟶	Build uniformity and reliability
Training and education	⟶	Licensed machine operator for basic maintenance

out resorting to complicated maintenance management software installations. American manufacturers need to move away from the mentality of "Operators make it; maintenance fixes it." In the same way that TQC changes the attitude toward quality and the roles of quality assurance groups, TPM impacts the maintenance area. Maintenance needs to be a group effort involving management, engineers, maintenance personnel, and operators. Only then can greater profits and a superior manufacturing culture be achieved.

CHAPTER 11

EMPLOYEE INVOLVEMENT IN
THE QUALITY PROCESS

Joseph J. Gufreda
Larry A. Maynard
Lucy N. Lytle

World-class companies know that it no longer is enough to merely satisfy customers; rather, customers must become excited about products and services. Satisfied customers may try to find a better product, but excited customers extol products and services. *There is little chance that your customers will be excited about your products or services unless your workers are.* Employee involvement (EI) results in excited and committed workers.

Involvement means that every person has two jobs: doing his or her own job and improving the way the job is done (i.e., improving the system). Traditionally, most people were expected just to maintain the system rather than improve it. For example, engineers have been expected to engineer only, not to improve the way engineering is done.

Most executives already have heard about employee involvement; some may be aware of the extraordinary gains in quality, productivity, and employee morale to which it leads. EI is the most significant contribution made by the great Japanese companies to the quality movement. In fact, continuous improvement through employee involvement is the credo of many of these firms.

However, those not familiar with the subject may misunderstand or question the need for it. Contrary to what some think, EI involves more than simply organizing a few quality control circles or worker teams. Teams are an important component of EI, but they are only part of the picture. EI is the process of transforming an organization's culture to utilize the creative energies of *all* employees for problem solving and for making improvements.

More than a few American companies have jumped on the EI bandwagon, but have enjoyed only modest benefits. A key reason for this is that managers did not really expect employees to improve things that were important to management. Realizing this, employees felt that EI was just "fluff" to appease them. They felt manipulated. Effective involvement requires that people perceive that they are doing something that improves the business.

Institutionalizing a culture based on continuous improvement requires a significant investment in time and resources. Employees must be trained to use new skills, given time to learn them, and encouraged to apply them on the job. Support and guidance must be provided throughout the process. On the average, 5 to 10 percent of people's time should be allocated for team activities, including training, meetings, and education. Eventually, the number of ideas generated and the percentage of these ideas implemented become important measures of both individual and team performance.

EI has a number of advantages over traditional management systems:

- It replaces the adversarial "us versus them" mentality with trust, cooperation, and common goals.
- It helps develop individual capability by improving self-management and leadership skills, creating a sense of mission, and fostering trust.
- It increases employee morale and commitment.
- It fosters creativity and innovation, the source of competitive advantage.
- It helps people understand quality principles and instills these principles into the corporate culture.

- It allows employees to solve problems at the source immediately.
- It improves quality and productivity.
- It makes good business sense since two heads are better than one when it comes to identifying and solving problems.
- It is the dominant organizational model among world-class companies.

Studies have shown that the decision to change from a traditional management system to one based on quality principles is two to ten times more effective when made by a group as a whole than when exhorted by an individual lecturer. Giving a group responsibility for their own goals and procedures truly maximizes the increase in productivity and morale.

EI is the key to maintaining momentum in a quality improvement process. It provides increased flexibility and adaptability to changes in the marketplace, customer needs, competition, and governmental regulations. Workers must be viewed as renewable resources, inherently more adaptable than new equipment or technology. Continuously upgrading quality requires that people be continually upgraded and cultivated, both personally and professionally.

JOB FUNCTIONS REDEFINED

To reap maximum benefits from an employee involvement initiative, all levels of the organization—top management, middle management, and work force—must be involved in one of two ways: through team activities or through individual activities supporting a quality team or related to a job function.

As the EI process is absorbed into the culture, many of the roles, responsibilities, and activities of individuals and departments begin to overlap. The organization will "de-layer" and compress. Responsibility for judgments, decisions, and problem resolution will then shift downward to those closest to the point of activity.

Top Management's Role

Top management must focus on creating a vision of the future state of the company, developing a change strategy to attain the vision, and then deploying the vision and strategy throughout the organization via policy deployment (PD). In order to do this, top management needs to balance the company's short-term needs with its long-term objectives and to be actively involved in overcoming cultural barriers and in assessing the development of the quality improvement effort. Top management's role, in essence, is to create alignment between individual and business needs. The *only* way to do this is to "walk-the-talk," that is, to epitomize the right leadership behavior.

The changes in responsibility resulting from overlapped activities may be difficult for an organization to absorb. At all levels, people will struggle with the change in job functions. For top management, this means some traditional upper management activities must be shared and performed by middle management. For example, effective policy deployment requires a give-and-take process between upper and other management. Traditionally, upper management told middle management what to do and did not really want feedback other than, "Yes sir! Can do."

At the beginning of the quality process, top management should form a steering committee, also known as a quality implementation team or quality council, to oversee the team building process. Team leaders should report their group's activities to the steering committee, guide the overall process and offer support when needed. The committee is responsible for the following activities:

- Ensuring resources.
- Communicating the state of the business, total quality implementation plans, and progress with respect to plans.
- Providing education and training.
- Assessing progress.
- Ensuring recognition and rewards.

Middle Management's Role

Middle management plays several roles in the quality process: translating top management's vision, mission, and strategy into functional activities for the organization; providing feedback to top management concerning the status of the functional activities; and aligning top management's vision with the staff and the work force individual needs.

As self-managed and semiautonomous work teams assume some problem-solving responsibilities previously belonging to supervisors and middle managers, the latter may feel threatened by the erosion of their traditional roles. Rather than making all the decisions and telling people what to do, managers are now asked to create an environment that encourages all employees to problem solve and to make improvements. This transition to a more self-directed system is one of the most difficult cultural changes a company must make, particularly for those managers who have advanced successfully through the traditional, top-down system.

Traditional culture assumed that managers were aware and in control of every problem. Consequently, managers consciously or unconsciously discouraged subordinates from bringing up problems they did not know about because it implied that they were not in control. Being sensitive to what the boss wants, employees kept problems to themselves for fear of evoking the boss's wrath.

Existing adversarial relationships often intensified when management refused to share business or competitive information with the workers, assuming that they either had no right to know or that these were matters about which they would not be interested. Unfortunately, not only did these practices intensify the sense of "us versus them," but they also prevented the work force from fully identifying with the company.

In contrast, the new quality model demonstrates that managers cannot realistically be expected to be aware of every problem and that those working closest to the system are usually in the best position to analyze and improve it. Managers should encourage workers to identify problem and improvement areas and, as far as possible, empower these people to implement solutions. Continuous improvement requires problem solving, which can only occur in an environment where employees can express problems openly and without fear of reprisal.

Actually, it is much easier to be open about what is going on than to be closed and to have to explain why certain decisions have been made. When people understand the situation as management does, they usually reach the same conclusion. Management should be open with employees about the bad, as well as good, news. An open attitude builds trust, an essential condition for overcoming people's fears about the quality-related changes sweeping through the organization, and encourages experimentation and cooperation. Only after employees understand where their company stands in terms of profit and loss, market share, competition, etc., can they develop a sense of mission about becoming a world-class competitor.

The traditional organizational model is a pyramid, with the work force comprising the widest part and middle management sandwiched between the work force and the executive suite at the top (see Figure 1). One way to visualize the new model is to invert this pyramid (see Figure 2). This inversion illustrates that in one sense the most important people in an organization are the line workers—those people manufacturing the products

FIGURE 1
Traditional Organizational Model

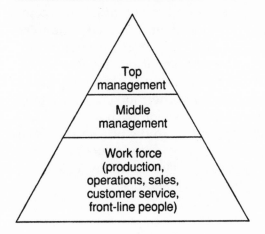

FIGURE 2
New Organizational Model

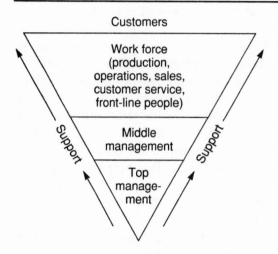

and/or serving the customers—and managers should function primarily as a resource to the line, offering equal amounts of support and guidance in their new roles as planners, coaches, and facilitators.

Most managers make the transition to their new roles successfully if given enough time and support. However, even staunch champions of the change may find themselves slipping into old patterns on occasion, as did one company's senior vice-president. As a member of the quality implementation team (steering committee) responsible for managing his company's quality process, this executive encouraged employee suggestions—until they affected his area. When a work team, formed to assemble a series of recommendations for increasing communication about quality, suggested that the company make a videotape, he suddenly began to resist their ideas. After a long and, according to bystanders, loud discussion with a consultant, the vice-president realized his opposition to the project stemmed from the fact that this particular quality idea was not his. After realizing this, he gave his approval. The company has since produced several extremely effective videotapes.

The Role of the Work Force

Members of the work force generally accept the quality process and genuinely welcome its changes and increased responsibility. Most are aching to be listened to for a change. They have a renewed sense of their importance to the organization and an increased understanding of their role in producing and delivering quality products and services.

There are two types of EI teams: cross-functional and family. Cross-functional teams perform a specific task or work on the continual improvement of a cross-functional business process (e.g., a new service design or new employee selection). Members come from different disciplines and functional areas, as well as from all organizational levels. Teams focused on a specific task usually disband when their project is completed. By comparison, family teams include individuals within a functional area or department, and, typically, the supervisor of the area serves as team leader. Family teams exist indefinitely, although team members may change over time. Ideally, 100 percent of employees will become involved in team activities.

Initially, team participation by the work force should be voluntary. Over time, however, all persons should be expected to contribute. World-class companies depend upon employees who want to improve the processes in which they work. For this reason and because so much will be invested in employees, the new employee selection process is extremely critical.

There are four types of team members, as discussed in the following:

1. *Leader*—He or she conducts meetings, provides direction, assesses progress, interfaces with other teams and support resources, and represents the group to management. Desirable leadership qualities include the ability to listen and to accept others' ideas, tolerance for human imperfection, enthusiasm, helpfulness, ability to focus, and sensitivity. A team's first leader is usually the highest level supervisor or manager on that team. In time, however, other team members can and should assume the leadership role.

2. *Facilitator*—Although the team leader focuses on identifying and solving problems, the facilitator, who can be a member of any company division, concentrates on the process for doing these things. His or her primary role is to help the leader. He or she is also responsible for seeking opinions, coordinating different ideas, testing consensus, applying tools and techniques, summarizing key points, and generally providing feedback to the group. The facilitator should elicit the opinions of the less vocal members and make certain that powerful personalities do not dominate the proceedings. In short, he or she must help the team to accomplish their goals while developing both individual and collective capabilities, primarily by helping the team leader.

3. *Trainer*—Often an outside consultant assumes initial responsibility for training employees in quality improvement techniques, problem solving, leadership, and facilitation skills. Eventually, however, employees should assume this function. Ideally, managers will be the first trainers—an excellent way for managers to lead by example.

4. *Participants*—Participants are responsible for recommending meeting agenda items, offering their perspective and ideas, performing assignments, ensuring that decisions and follow-up assignments are clear, and helping to critique and improve the meeting process. Particularly during pilot projects, team members should be selected carefully. Ideally, these people will be volunteers who are committed to improving quality, who identify with the team's goals, who are cooperative team players, and who possess the capability to become leaders and/or facilitators.

Employee involvement transforms front-line employees into teams of problem identifiers and solvers, responsibilities previously reserved mostly for managers. This is a revolutionary redefinition of roles, yet one that makes practical sense since those closest to problems are the ones who now must solve them.

Consider one consultant's experience working with a glue operation at a manufacturing company. As a result of an EI project, one team member was put in charge of filling glue bottles for the line. After opening a new drum, the employee noticed that the glue was lumpy and separated and that the operators had to shake the glue bottles before using them. The employee immediately pulled the bottles containing the new glue from the line and conducted a series of time-phased tests attempting to glue two pieces of material together. Even after being under pressure for two hours, the glue would not set. The worker then notified management that there was a problem, management ordered a new glue container. As a result, several units were saved from field failure. Soon after, the team reconvened to develop new procedures for glue testing before it was used in production. They also worked with the glue supplier to eliminate future problems. This type of employee initiative is critical to becoming a world-class competitor.

Effective teams are concerned with both results/tasks and the meeting process (i.e., how meetings are managed, problems are solved, decisions are made, and goals are accomplished). Some simple techniques to improve meetings include starting and ending the meeting on time, establishing an agenda ahead of time, distributing minutes from the previous meeting, taking time at the end of the meeting to discuss the meeting's effectiveness, and appointing a recorder to keep a running summary of decisions made, action items, and a timetable for completing these items.

It is often the highest paid people in a company, the executives whose days are spent in meetings, who benefit the most from focusing on the process of holding meetings. While they may be knowledgeable about forecasting business trends or analyzing market share, chances are that they never were taught how to run a meeting efficiently.

Pilot Projects

Education and training (detailed in Chapter 7) are key components of EI. The pilot projects give a small number of select teams the opportunity to apply the newly learned concepts and techniques in an on-the-job situation. In initial implementation efforts, three or four teams conduct pilot projects lasting three to six months. This duration is sufficient to commit to the process and to achieve considerable results, but not so long that momentum slows.

Ideally, the pilot project will have the following character-istics:

- It is within the group's span of control.
- It is manageable (i.e., "improve the order entry process" is an appropriate assignment whereas "eliminate the long-standing communication problem between two divisions" is too nebulous and large in scope).
- It is something that most team members feel will help them perform their jobs better.
- It can be implemented quickly.
- It is measurable/tangible.
- It is important to management.

All work teams will eventually have their own projects. Overtime is usually required in the beginning to provide training and to allow the teams to learn new skills.

After awhile, time saved by the teams' efforts can be reinvested—more teams can be formed. Successful pilots educate and motivate other teams. The rate of expansion of the number of work teams is a function of the degree to which a company possesses the following:

- Leadership to direct, support, and inspire the process.
- Facilitation to ensure that the leadership is consistent with the new model.
- Knowledge of what to do and how to do it.
- Will and energy to act.
- Time and resources to effect lasting changes.

Life Cycle of a Team

Understanding a team's life cycle is as important as understanding a product's life cycle. Managers unfamiliar with this process may have unreasonable expectations for teams and demand immediate results before teams have had time to gel. Normally, the life cycle of a team has three phases.

1. *Build*—At this stage, team members may feel uneasy and unsure of what to do. Team leaders and facilitators should

help to clarify people's expectations and work to overcome their initial apprehension.

2. *Develop*—During this phase, teams gain momentum. Because relationships will be evolving, conflicts may arise. This is to be expected and should not be used as an excuse for abandoning team efforts.

3. *Optimize*—At this point, the team has gelled and works together more effectively. The leaders and facilitators play a less active role as the team manages itself.

Most individuals have a fundamental need to belong and, given the chance, will eagerly contribute to an organization's growth and success. When employees feel a sense of ownership in the process and pride in their accomplishments, their thinking shifts from how much they do or how hard they work to how much they know and can contribute to the organization's well-being. These changes build company loyalty while instilling confidence in the goals and purpose of the organization.

CREATIVITY: A KEY TO SUCCESS

The success of many work teams lies in unlocking employees' innate creativity and applying it to existing problems within the organization. Therefore it is recommended that team training include exercises that foster creativity. Human beings are naturally creative, but they often suppress this ability in the process of moving toward adulthood. It is not uncommon for adults to dismiss their imaginative abilities; but, when was the last time someone heard a five year old reject a pot of fingerpaint because "I'm not a creative person"?

Fear is the primary block to creativity: fear of making a mistake, of looking like a fool, of being criticized, of disturbing traditions, of losing the love and support of a group, and so on. Discovery is the process of looking at the same thing everyone else is eyeing and seeing something different.

One consultant, the father of three, explains the process of losing creativity this way:

> When my youngest son, Matt, who is four, brings home a drawing of a red blob with green appendages and shows it to me, the first

thing I do is compliment him on his handiwork. When he explains that it is an elephant, I nod and assure him that I knew that all along. When my daughter, Andrea, who is two years older, brings me a similar drawing, I compliment her, too, but I also take the opportunity to point out that elephants are gray, not green and red. Finally, when my oldest son, Joey, presents the same drawing, I admire it, then get on the phone to his teacher to demand why a nine year old hasn't learned how to draw a proper elephant yet. The point is that by stifling people's creativity, we end up in a world filled with dull gray elephants. [See Figure 3.]

One useful exercise to illustrate how people block their own creativity is the "nine-dot" exercise. Participants are shown a square formed of three rows of three dots each, as shown in Figure 4, and asked to connect all of the dots using four lines or fewer and without lifting their pencils off the page. One way to connect all nine dots is to extend two of the lines beyond the implicit boundaries suggested by the square. Another solution, offered by a particularly enterprising individual, is to use a very fat pencil to cover all the dots at once. This exercise is an excellent way to teach people to recognize the limits they unconsciously impose on themselves.

FIGURE 3

FIGURE 4
The Nine-Dot Exercise

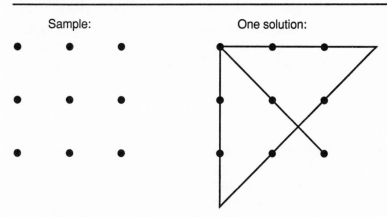

Sample: One solution:

RECOGNITION AND REWARD
IN THE QUALITY PROCESS

Recognition and reward are the best means of connecting accomplishments with positive feedback.

Recognition may come in the form of top management's acknowledgement of team activities or of articles in the company newspaper lauding individual and team accomplishments. A brief note from a top executive thanking someone for his or her efforts can have a tremendous impact on employee morale. Rewards can be monetary or they can be nominal, such as hats, mugs, or jackets. Monetary rewards offered by most world-class companies for improvement ideas usually do not exceed several hundred dollars. In these companies, the larger monetary rewards usually are given to the person having the greatest number of ideas, to someone who has a "breakthrough" idea, or to members of the team that has made the greatest contribution.

One company realized the importance of recognition when it established a cross-functional team to study and develop reward and recognition programs for the organization. They discovered that the company newspaper, which had been cut back due to economics, had been very popular with employees, many of whom had saved editions in their desks for up to 30 years. The team recommended that the company paper be resurrected, redesigned, and revitalized to serve as the primary vehicle of recognition. Additionally, the hallway leading to the cafeteria was dedicated to team efforts, with pictures and other signs of accomplishment prominently displayed. This display area communicated results and recognized performance.

CONCLUSION

Involving employees in the quality process requires budgeting time for them to be educated/trained and to spend time actually solving problems and making improvements. This contrasts with the traditional approach of maintaining only minimal direct labor to support known demand and allowing only management and some indirect personnel to work on improving the process.

Traditionally, American businesses have failed to express their purpose and goals in terms that inspire their people. To continue to succeed in the new era of quality requires managers to redefine how they think of and treat their employees. Successful executives will work to unlock the human potential existing in their organizations to forge the strongest and best competitive weapon of the future. Perhaps nothing illustrates this point as powerfully as a casual remark made by team members of many companies: "This is the first time in the eight years I've been with the company that I actually looked forward to coming to work."

PART 3

EXECUTING STRATEGY

CHAPTER 12

JIT AND QUALITY

Steven M. Ray

Many well-intentioned programs, aimed at achieving competitive advantage through just-in-time (JIT), have met with failure and disappointment. Managers have been misled regarding the meaning of JIT and the actions required to become world class. Most still view JIT as synonymous with zero inventories and pull production.

The problem lies in the translation of JIT ideals into required actions. Consider the following ideals:

- An O.E.M. supplier makes daily deliveries directly to customers' production lines. The quantity delivered equals the quantity consumed since the last delivery.
- Produce only what is needed and when it is needed to satisfy customer needs. Do not build any inventory in anticipation of future demands.
- Synchronize all internal production operations and produce only in response to consumption at the next immediate downstream operation, one at a time (i.e., pull production).
- Maintain a high degree of flexibility to changes in volume, mix, and design.
- Receive daily deliveries from world-class suppliers direct to the production line.
- Achieve all the previous ideals at less cost than the competition.

Ideals, by definition, serve as a mental image of a standard of perfection or excellence. The ideals previously listed serve as a model of the perfect JIT environment, one that may never be fully realized. The purpose of ideals is to guide actions, to move one ever closer to achieving the ideals.

Determining the actions required demands an understanding of the fundamental concepts and principles of the JIT philosophy. Here lies the heart of the problem. Training has been weak on underlying concepts; instead, it has focused on various techniques for achieving pull production. The association of ideals and techniques, without establishing a staunch understanding of underlying concepts and principles, has led to deception and misguided programs. Implement the following techniques—cellular manufacturing, balanced operations, JIT deliveries—and become a world-class manufacturer, or so it might seem. A perfunctory review of JIT may easily lead to such conclusions.

JIT is the basic philosophy and the core component of manufacturing excellence. The JIT philosophy is based on the two principles of *continuous improvement* and *elimination of waste*—continuous improvement in productivity, quality, customer service, and flexibility in product design and schedule changes, and elimination of any activity that does not add value to product or service. JIT requires total quality control (TQC). Without quality improvement, there is no JIT.

So what is the relationship between inventory and JIT? pull production and JIT? What actions are required, if not these? Where does quality improvement fit in? The answers to these questions are the subject of this chapter.

INVENTORY—AN ABSOLUTE EVIL

In the United States, inventory has been considered a necessary evil due to a misunderstanding of the fundamental need for improvement. Inventory exists for a reason and has been used to counter the impact of unreliable marketing, design, and production systems. Rather than identifying and eliminating root causes of problems, U.S. manufacturers have hidden the problems with inventory. Are your customers demanding shorter lead time than manufacturing cycle times will allow? Better build some inventory! Are you having difficulty with production yields? Make sure there is plenty in work-in-process! These are common examples of the uses of inventory in the United States.

World-class companies consider inventory to be an absolute evil. In fact, it is the root of all evil. Their version of JIT is aimed at eliminating inventory by eliminating the root causes that create the need for inventory. They understand that production without inventory is achieved only through fundamental improvement in the total system, from marketing and design through production and shipment.

PULL PRODUCTION

Pull production by itself does nothing to fundamentally improve systems and processes. It is simply a technique for controlling production. Those who attempt to implement pull production without first substantially improving the reliability of the total production system are likely to fail. Some may have limited success, especially those whose processes are characterized as simple, as employing mature technologies, or as requiring little precision in manufacturing or product specifications. However, they will fall well short of achieving the ideals of JIT.

Certain conditions should exist before any attempt is made to implement pull production. In general, pull production requires repetitiveness and fixed routings (i.e., only one sequence of operations is used to manufacture a given product, part, or set of parts). However, it is difficult to discern when these conditions have been met because it is a matter of degree. If each was plotted on a continuum from low to high indicating the degree to which the condition had been met, two things would be evident. First, if all conditions have been met only to low degree, any attempt at pull production will meet with failure. Second, all conditions must be satisfied to a high degree to achieve the ideals. A review of these conditions will point out the importance of improving pull production and other JIT ideals.

Repetitiveness

Laying out the factory into cells or flow lines will require a degree of repetitiveness sufficient to justify dedicating equipment. Nearly all companies have some degree of repetitiveness. The Pareto principle applies almost universally. In some cases, a small number of products represent the lion's share of production volume. In others, it may be a family of products. In still others, it may not relate to products at all, but to processes. One manufacturer of precision metal components found that, although no single product or family of products represented significant volume, over 90 percent of his products went through a similar process. He had forever utilized the traditional clustered organization of equipment, moving material from department to department, all the while thinking he was a job shop. After two years of intensive efforts to improve processes and quality, a pull production system was implemented, reducing throughput time from a week to a day. It is easy to assume you are a job shop, especially if you operate like one.

Just as there are few "pure" job shops, few manufacturers are totally repetitive. Consequently, not all products can be manufactured utilizing a pull production system. Efforts to implement pull production, therefore, should concentrate on those "vital few" products representing the bulk of total volume. These products are repetitive and their routings can be fixed. The remaining products, often referred to as the "trivial many," are best controlled under traditional methods, although attention should still be given to improving production systems and to minimizing inventory and throughput time.

Capable Processes

Widely fluctuating operation yields will make it impossible to balance a production line, resulting in excessive idle time in a pull production system. When yields at a given operation are greater than planned, the operator will be able to replenish inventory at the next downstream operation faster than it will be consumed, causing all upstream operations to shut down. If yields are less than planned, inventory will not be replenished quickly enough, resulting in idle time for all downstream operations. Production will be jittery at best.

Pull production can be implemented successfully in processes exhibiting low but *predictable* yields, where operations are in statistical control, but with variation exceeding that required to consistently meet specifications. In this situation, operations are balanced assuming a certain percentage of time lost due to scrap, while inventory buffers between operations are kept high enough to absorb the random variation in yield.

Achieving the ideals of producing only what is needed when needed and producing one at a time demands high process capability. Becoming a certified supplier requires the ability to manufacture, not inspect, quality into products.

This author's experience implementing pull production at Hutchinson Technology, Inc. (HTI), points out the importance of process capability to pull production. HTI manufactures various components and assemblies for original equipment manufacturers in the computer peripherals market. The company is divided into six distinct product groups. Having succeeded in implementing pull production in four of the six product groups, and having reduced throughput time in some instances to less than two hours, the company decided to forge ahead and implement it in another area.

The process was characterized as pushing the envelope in technology, that is, employing relatively new production techniques. Process yields fluctuated widely from week to week. Average yields from one week to the next sometimes differed as much as 20 percentage points. This area also experienced significant downtime due to variation in raw material and to equipment and tooling malfunctions.

Implementing pull production with this product line initially resulted in a reduction of throughput time from ten weeks to five days accompanied by a drastic cut in work-in-process inventory. However, several unexpected problems emerged. Not only was there significant idle time and lost output, but the process required constant attention. As products were pulled through the process, the mix was governed by starts at the first operation. As yields fluctuated, the schedule of starts had to be adjusted to control the mix. Also, when yields were low, the additional start quantities had to be expedited through the process to meet ship dates. Line balancing was not only impossible, but the bottleneck shifted day-to-day, which compounded scheduling problems further.

Eventually, inventory was allowed to build at certain operations, and the need to return to traditional means of dispatching product was recognized. Despite this temporary reversal, pull production continues to be an area objective, although the need to improve process capability first remains.

In contrast, HTI successfully implemented pull production in processes with yields as low as 80 percent. In one such process, throughput was reduced from one week to eight hours with minimal idle time or other disruption. Success, relative to the prior example, is attributed to consistent, predictable yields and to the overall reliability of the total production system.

Stable Schedules

The ultimate vision of pull production is to make product on demand at precisely the same rate and mix at which orders are received. If 1,000 orders are received one day, 1,000 products will be made that day. If 3,000 orders are received, 3,000 products will be made. Economically, to do this requires an extremely high degree of flexibility. Even for the best of the world-class companies, this capability is still in the future, and to effectively balance operations and pull products through the factory, most companies must have a constant schedule of production requirements for some period of time. Unless the customer demand pattern is already smooth, this means maintaining some finished goods inventories to allow sporadic shipments, while leveling internal production requirements.

The period of time that the schedule needs to be leveled depends upon cumulative production throughput time, which is a reflection of the current flexibility to proauct design and schedule changes. Upon hearing that world-class producers level their schedules, some manufacturers discount the achievements, claiming that their own customers would not stand for it. These traditionalists change schedules daily in the immediate time frame, resulting in chaos, poor quality, and missed schedules. Leveling the schedule for a period of time that reflects the organization's current flexibility is an essential requirement for becoming world class. Paradoxically, companies must stabilize the schedule to allow the organization to improve flexibility.

Traditional inventory management methods employ lot-sizing techniques that create lumpy demands. Economic order quantity (EOQ) formulas, for instance, calculate the most "economic" quantity given a trade-off between ordering (e.g., setup) and carrying costs of inventory. Therefore, even if demand in the end market is uniform, manufacturers throughout the supply chain may be distorting demand for economy's sake.

However, searching for economies is not an issue. The problem lies in assuming ordering costs are fixed while underestimating the cost of carrying inventory. The challenge is to convince others in the supply chain of the need to reduce ordering costs and to use an inventory carrying cost of at least 48 percent to compensate for the many hidden costs of inventory. As carrying costs rise and ordering costs decline, the EOQ approaches zero and lumpy demand subsides.

Reliable Tooling and Equipment

In a JIT environment, inventory no longer exists to compensate for protracted tooling and equipment repair. Equipment and tooling failures translate into work stoppages; therefore, a high degree of reliability is essential.

Reliability is enhanced through problem solving and preventive maintenance. When equipment and tooling failures are experienced, root causes must be found and permanent solutions must be implemented. Too frequently, repairs are made again and again without investigation of causes.

As described in a previous chapter, total productive maintenance (TPM) is a system for improving the process capability and effectiveness of all equipment. TPM goes beyond preventive- and predictive-maintenance approaches designed simply to avoid breakdowns. Zero breakdowns is not enough; the goals of TPM are to improve process capability and to maximize equipment effectiveness. Often this requires design revisions and modifications to existing equipment and tooling.

Capability, reliability, ease of use and maintenance, and flexibility are all paramount issues when designing/redesigning tooling and equipment.

Short Setup Times

Small lot sizes, short throughput times, and the flexibility to rapidly change from one product or part to another demand quick and accurate setups. The ideal state is the one-touch setup, which can be performed without affecting cycle time through the operation. For most companies, reaching this ideal is unfathomable. However, there are many examples of companies reducing complex setups from hours to minutes and even seconds, and an abundance of literature describes effective setup reduction techniques. A 50 percent reduction, at little or no cost, is common for first-time attempts to reduce setup time. After several repetitions, many companies have even experienced reductions in excess of 90 percent.

The advantages of pull production are greatly diminished when setup times are great. Lot sizes must remain high to avoid labor costs, while inventory buffers between operations must be significant to minimize disruption of line balance while setups are being performed. However, despite these limitations, traditional methods of controlling production are no better. The object is to institute a continuing program for setup reduction to permit reductions in lot sizes and inventory buffers, not to reduce overall setup costs. These reductions in lot sizes and inventory buffers result in shorter throughput time and increased flexibility.

Immediate Feedback and Response to Problems

In a world-class JIT environment there is very little inventory to fall back on. This situation requires that everything be done correctly the first and every time. Therefore, reliability and consistency throughout the total production system are imperative.

To ensure that things are done correctly the first time, workers must be trained to assess quality at the source and they must be empowered to shut down an operation when problems are encountered. Problems must be addressed immediately so the evidence is fresh, and support personnel (e.g., quality engineering, process engineering, and production maintenance) must be conditioned to respond quickly, often within minutes of the event. If the solution is not apparent, a decision may be made to keep running—sorting or reworking bad product later—while problem-solving efforts continue. The greater sins are to ignore problems altogether or to disregard evidence vital to generating solutions. As solutions are found, efforts must then be devoted to fail-safing the process to prevent reoccurrence of problems.

World-Class Suppliers

Purchased material can represent as much as 70–90 percent of product costs. Given this heavy reliance on external suppliers, it is not enough to improve internal processes only. The concepts of manufacturing excellence must be extended to suppliers, from suppliers to their suppliers, and so on throughout the entire supply chain. The influence suppliers have on a company's ability to improve product and service quality is too great to be ignored.

In the ideal JIT environment, pull production is extended to suppliers as if they were extensions of a company's own processes. Suppliers deliver daily and directly to the production line, bypassing incoming inspection since quality is assured. They manufacture and deliver only what is needed, when it is needed. The same degree of reliability throughout the supplier's processes is required to achieve this ideal.

Building a world-class supplier base is not an easy task. To start, a company must stop awarding business on the basis of price alone. It must align itself with suppliers sharing a commitment to manufacturing excellence. Then, all must work together for mutual gain. Chapter 14 is devoted entirely to strategies for building a world-class supplier base.

THE QUALITY THREAD

The degree of success in achieving the ideals of JIT manufacturing depends on the extent to which the previously described conditions are satisfied. Satisfying these conditions is a quality issue since the actions required must focus on fundamental improvement in the capability and reliability of the total production system. It is through quality improvement that an environment conducive to world-class JIT performance is created.

Quality relates to every action. When A.V. Feigenbaum wrote his book, *Total Quality Control,* he pointed out that quality is an issue for all functions and activities (e.g., manufacturing, engineering, marketing, finance). Everyone must endeavor to satisfy customer needs, to achieve reliability and consistency in all processes, to reduce variation, and to improve continuously. Customers are not only external customers, but are also the next people in the process. Processes relate not only to production, but also to all surrounding activities. In this sense, equipment malfunction or failure to respond immediately to operating problems are as much quality issues as processes incapable of producing product within specification.

It is important to understand what is meant by "fundamental improvement" and "total production systems." Production in large lot sizes was once considered improvement because it led to lower labor costs, and allocated long, expensive setups over more units. However, it also led to higher inventory, longer cycle times, increased investment, and other problems that diminished the economies sought. Increase in lot sizes is not a fundamental improvement. Fundamental improvement involves reducing or eliminating setup, thereby reducing labor costs without trade-offs. Inspection was once considered a means to improve quality. However, manufacturers merely avoided sending bad product to customers. In fact, there was no fundamental improvement in processes to avoid defects in the first place. To achieve fundamental improvement, root causes must be identified. To eliminate them, the disease must be treated, not the symptoms.

The total production system refers to an entire manufacturing enterprise, including all of the functions (marketing, engineering, production, finance). Improvement focused only on production operations does little to improve production activities as a whole. Essential functions, both production and administrative, must be identified and every element of those functions must be improved relentlessly.

Quality improvement is essential for improved reliability which, in turn, is essential to achieving the ideals of JIT. Therefore, quality improvement must receive top priority. Without quality improvement, there is no JIT. Again, Hutchinson Technology, Inc., is a startling example. While many manufacturers have struggled for years to implement pull production and other JIT "techniques" with only meager success, in a span of just a few months, HTI implemented pull production systems throughout 80 percent of all production operations. Finished-goods turns now exceed 130. Work-in-process turns increased from 18 to 70. Raw-material turns went from 2 to 12, while maintaining a 99 percent service level. In one product line, manufacturing throughput decreased from two weeks to two hours. These are only a few examples of a long list of achievements accomplished in a short time period.

The principal reason for HTI's rapid success was a major quality-improvement initiative, which had been launched two years earlier. Massive effort and resources had been committed to educating and training all employees in TQC and to managing the transformation. All employee levels had become committed to measuring and improving quality throughout all processes.

Simply put, the reliability of the total production system had improved substantially, removing many of the barriers to inventory reduction and simplified production methods.

AN INTEGRATED APPROACH

This chapter has attempted to guide those who have a repetitive environment, think JIT is synonymous with pull production, and want to jump into it immediately. Without quality improvement, any attempt to implement pull production, except in the simplest of environments, is likely to fail. Even if successful, attaining the JIT ideals would be nearly impossible unless there existed an ongoing effort to improve reliability throughout the total production system.

Many techniques embedded in JIT should be applied, even though quality improvement has not progressed far enough to permit pull production. For instance, inventories should be reduced gradually as processes become more reliable. Workplace organization, housekeeping, and setup reduction are techniques frequently associated with JIT that do not require improved reliability of other processes, but that contribute to the reliability of the total production system. Ideally, application of JIT techniques is integrated with quality improvement.

Once the underlying JIT concepts are understood, actions and priorities become clearer. Achieving the ideals of JIT is the destination, reached by a journey of continuous, fundamental improvement and elimination of waste. Actions centered around companywide quality improvement are the fuels that propel us on that journey.

CHAPTER 13

COST MANAGEMENT
SYSTEMS, JIT, AND QUALITY

Robert D. McIlhattan

INTRODUCTION

The total quality and just-in-time (JIT) philosophies are reshaping the physical nature of the production environment. They are also changing both the behavioral patterns of production costs and how financial executives must measure and control these costs. Some of the changes being applied by financial executives to traditional cost management systems to make them more consistent with the total quality and JIT philosophies need to be studied and, perhaps, emulated by others.

Each of the changes discussed have been practiced by organizations successfully by applying total quality and JIT to their businesses. They realized that changes in their cost management systems were necessary to keep pace with the process changes resulting from the adoption of total quality.

The total quality philosophy is creating manufacturing environments that require a new, more innovative means of approaching cost management. Traditional methods and procedures for measuring and reporting production costs begin to erode in a total quality environment and require changing existing cost management systems. For example, JIT will significantly impact the following:

- Identification of cost drivers.
- Number of product cost elements.
- Application of product costs.
- Nature of performance measures.

A number of organizations have enhanced their cost management systems to complement JIT methods. While specific solutions have varied from one organization to another, there are common elements within all solutions.

INDICATION OF COST DRIVERS

Perhaps the greatest impact of JIT on an organization's cost management system is that it focuses management's attention on *nonvalue*-added processes. A nonvalue-added process is any activity or procedure performed within a company that does not add value to a product.

For example, assume the lead time associated with manufacturing a salable product generally comprises the following steps:

- *Process time* is the amount of time a product is actually being worked on.
- *Inspection time* is the amount of time spent either assuring the product's high quality or reworking the product to an acceptable quality level.
- *Move time* is the time spent moving the product from one location to another.
- *Queue time* is the amount of time the product waits before being processed, moved, inspected, etc.
- *Storage time* is the amount of time a product spends in stock before further processing or shipment.

Of these five steps, only process time actually adds value to the product. All other activities—inspection time, move time, queue time, and storage time—add cost but no value and, therefore, are deemed as *nonvalue-added* processes within the total quality philosophy.

In many organizations, process time is much less than 10 percent of the total manufacturing lead time and cost associated with manufacturing a salable item. Costs associated with longer lead times include shortages, obsolescence, and expediting. Therefore, over 90 percent of the manufacturing lead time associated with a product adds cost, but no value to the product. It is this premise that leads to the total quality philosophy that reducing lead time will reduce total cost.

To assist in this process, financial executives in JIT environments have identified some causes for the time and cost associated with the nonvalue-added elements of a manufacturing process.

The key impact on traditional cost accounting is that cost management systems now need to identify the cause of costs—the "cost drivers"—in addition to capturing the resultant costs. Harley Davidson, Omark Industries, Hewlett-Packard, and other successful JIT users have undertaken studies to define the true "drivers" associated with increasing costs (see Figure 1 for a list of "cost drivers").

In all cases, the organization determined there was a direct correlation between the number of transactions and the cost of production. In addition, Hewlett-Packard determined that many costs were a direct function of the number of vendors used, the number of engineering changes to the product, and the total number of part numbers it maintained.

FIGURE 1
Potential Cost Drivers

Number of labor transactions

Number of material moves

Number of total part numbers

Number of parts received in a month

Number of part numbers in an average product

Number of products

Average number of options

Number of schedule changes

Number of accessories

Number of vendors

Number of units scrapped

Number of engineering change notices

Number of process changes

Number of units reworked

Number of direct labor employees

Number of new parts introduced

Product and process cycle time

Business process cycle time (e.g., order processing time)

By refocusing the cost management system to identify the true force behind nonvalue-added activities, financial executives were able to assist the manufacturing managers in eliminating product design and manufacturing process inefficiencies that were at the root of the product cost issues.

Product designs were simplified, reducing engineering changes and part numbers, which correspondingly reduced financial problems associated with excess stock, obsolescence, storages, rework, and other associated costs. Vendors were reduced, improving quality and delivery schedules. Reporting transactions were either eliminated completely (in the case of direct labor) or reduced to an absolute minimum, thereby eliminating support costs for clerical activities associated with transaction processing, error correction, waiting time, and moving time.

Through identification of the costs associated with nonvalue-added activities, financial executives in each organization have helped determine the true "drivers" of these activities and costs. Once identified, these drivers could be reduced or eliminated.

NUMBER OF PRODUCT COST ELEMENTS

One effect JIT is having on cost management systems is the reduction in the number of a product's cost elements. JIT, while applicable to virtually any industry or process, has the greatest success in industries where, because of the nature of their products and processes, standard cost systems have been adopted.

Most traditional standard cost systems maintain standard cost elements for material, direct labor, and manufacturing overhead. More sophisticated standard cost systems often maintain more than these elements. As a manager's need for better cost information increases, overhead costs are typically broken into more finite elements in order to control production costs. Standard product cost elements associated with variable overhead, fixed overhead, setup, material acquisition, energy, direct labor overhead, etc., are added to cost systems to obtain better visibility and control over product-related costs.

However, as explained previously, one of the primary philosophies of total quality is to identify the cost drivers associated with production costs. Once identified, continual improvement in the reduction of product cost through design and process improvements on a daily basis eliminates the need to define multiple cost elements.

Harley Davidson is an example of a JIT-dedicated organization that has reduced the number of standard cost elements associated with its products. It has converted from five cost elements per part (direct material, direct labor, setup, variable overhead, and fixed overhead) to only two (direct material and conversion cost). Similar changes have been made by many other JIT organizations, including IBM and Caterpillar.

The total quality and JIT philosophies have helped these organizations recognize that the issue is the elimination and prevention of costs, not simply the reporting of cost elements. The organizational acceptance and awareness that any cost, regardless of its nature, should be reduced, has focused attention on the fact that the design and process improvements necessary to implement JIT successfully will reduce cost through the enhancements themselves. Cost element reduction helps people focus on total product cost as opposed to individual elements. Additionally, the cost element reduction further reduces the support costs associated with their reporting, calculation, maintenance, and control.

It should be noted that while the number of product cost elements defined within the cost systems for JIT organizations declined, each retained its standard cost system so far. In fact, IBM is converting some facilities from a weighted average, actual cost system to a standard cost system. The application of the standard cost system has changed in that it is no longer used as widely to measure performance. The standard cost system, however, is still important as a tool for valuing inventory and cost of sales and as a tool to estimate potential future costs associated with design and/or process changes. Therefore, an additional effect of JIT is that standards are used more often as a tool to prevent costs before they arise, rather than to report against once the costs have been incurred. Again, fewer cost elements will suffice to meet their purpose.

APPLICATION OF PRODUCT COST

As stated, one of the key characteristics of JIT is the adoption of manufacturing cells dedicated to the production of single or similar products or major components. In addition to the primary objective of reducing manufacturing lead time, manufacturing cells also change the nature of product costs and introduce alternative methods of applying production costs to specific products flowing through each cell.

The vast majority of traditional cost-accounting systems in place today apply indirect manufacturing costs to products based on direct labor hours or dollars charged to a specific product. A JIT environment challenges this practice in two significant areas:

1. The vehicle used to charge and collect labor hours (or dollars) to a specific product in most traditional environments is the factory work order. As individuals work on specific jobs, they charge their time to the factory work order associated with the item being manufactured. Costs are, therefore, accumulated as the factory work order travels through the product process. Within a JIT environment, however, there may not be any factory work orders. Daily production schedules are provided for each cell, with only finished items reported by the cell over the day's course. No detail reporting is performed, again, consistent with the philosophy of reducing transactions and lead time. Therefore, the total of all related costs is applied to the day's production, not to individual jobs and tasks.

2. In a JIT environment, direct labor may not be correlated to other manufacturing costs and, as previously stated, is usually included in the total conversion costs. Within a JIT environment, alternative methods of applying cost to a product may be more appropriate. For example, many JIT users apply total conversion cost based on velocity through a manufacturing cell. Velocity is based on the theoretical number of units produced within a cell over a given period. Theoretical capacity is used because it is consistent with the total quality tenet of continual improvement toward perfection with no allowance for inefficiency or downtime. Based on velocity, a cost per hour is

computed for a given cell. Therefore, a day's production is costed simply by multiplying the number of units produced by the cost associated with the hours required to produce that day's production. Whether the hours were expended for direct labor, setup, queue, or machine hours, "time is money." The fact is that the longer it takes to produce something, the more it will cost.

Note that other application methods do exist, depending on the nature of the manufacturing cell process. These include material usage, equipment costs, or more imaginative terms identified as true cost drivers (e.g., number of transactions, quality, or number of engineering change orders).

A second major impact of JIT on applying product costs is the increase in production costs directly applicable to a product. This phenomenon is a function of the adoption of manufacturing cells and the dedication of those cells to single or similar products (see Figure 2).

A fundamental goal within a JIT environment is the reduction of total product cost. In order for the cost management system to measure success in this area, allocations must be eliminated to the greatest extent possible. As most financial executives are well aware, the greater the degree of allocations, the less reliable (or acceptable) the information is for decision-making purposes.

FIGURE 2.
Direct versus Indirect Costs

	Traditional Environment	*JIT Environment*
Direct labor	Direct	Direct
Material handling	Indirect	Direct
Repairs and maintenance	Direct	Direct
Energy	Indirect	Direct
Operating supplies	Indirect	Direct
Supervision	Indirect	Direct
Production support services	Indirect	Largely direct
Building occupancy	Indirect	Indirect
Insurance and taxes	Indirect	Indirect
Depreciation	Indirect	Direct

As illustrated in Figure 2, JIT helps eliminate allocations through the implementation of manufacturing cells dedicated to single or similar product production. However, many total quality organizations, including Harley Davidson, Omark, and IBM, have begun to adopt new cost management methods of associating total production costs (support function costs) directly with products in an effort to reduce allocations and to increase cost information reliability and responsibility (i.e., for 'ownership" of product costs).

For example, IBM has adopted the concept of directly cnarging costs to specific products as a result of their JIT enhancements. Costs are associated with products using one of three following methods:

1. Production floor expenses are charged directly to products as they flow through manufacturing cells.

2. Nonoccupancy-related support costs, such as cost accountancy and data processing, are "billed" directly to the products utilizing their services. The billing rates are negotiated between support-function managers and product managers before services are rendered and are based on the amount of support given to a specific product.

3. Occupancy-related costs are still allocated to products. Through the adoption of its direct charging approach, IBM has significantly increased the amount of support costs directly associated with a product without the need for allocations. Before this process was adopted, only 25 percent of support costs could be associated with a product. Today, 75 percent of all support costs can be associated with a product without allocation.

Comments by controllers who have adopted direct charging concepts indicate the benefit of enhancing JIT and resultant process changes. Controller comments include "Product manager's ownership of expense has improved"; "The accuracy of product cost is better"; "There is an increased visibility and awareness of expense items"; "It allows for flexibility in changing environment, improved sourcing decisions, and competitive analysis"; and "It allows for cost reductions and improves competitiveness."

THE NATURE OF PERFORMANCE MEASURES

As organizations begin to adopt a companywide commitment to total cost management, the performance measurements monitoring improvement and motivating personnel begin to change. Traditional measures, commonplace in many cost accounting systems, are not appropriate within the total quality philosophy of cost management. In fact, in some cases they may encourage actions contrary to the spirit of JIT. Four such examples are:

- Direct labor efficiency.
- Direct labor utilization.
- Direct labor productivity.
- Machine utilization.

These measurements are inappropriate for the following reasons:

1. They all promote building inventory beyond what is necessary for the immediate time frame.

2. Emphasizing performance to standard gives priority to output at the expense of quality. Relatively few companies even adjust results to reflect bad parts. Using standards for performance measurements can be limiting relative to continuous improvement. Once standards are attained, people usually feel they have "arrived."

3. Direct labor in the majority of companies accounts for only between 5 and 15 percent of total product cost. Traditional cost managers have run with tight direct labor control and relatively loose overhead control. Frequently, direct labor head count reductions have been more than offset by overhead increases.

4. Using machine utilization is similarly inappropriate because it encourages results in building inventory ahead of needs. Focusing on this measurement has frequently resulted in using expensive equipment and, sometimes, entire plants around the clock in the belief that this would maximize ROI. The fact is that under this scenario virtually no time is allowed for preventive maintenance; equipment is run flat out until it breaks down. When it does break down, there is considerable disruption, which ripples throughout manufacturing. This results in unnecessary costs and, in fact, the reduction in ROI instead of its maximization.

Figure 3 highlights some performance measures appropriate for a cost management system consistent with JIT and total quality.

FIGURE 3
Performance Measures: Traditional versus JIT/Total Quality

Traditional	JIT/Total Quality
Direct Labor	Total head count productivity —Output—total head
—Efficiency	count (direct, indirect, administrative personnel)
—Utilization	
—Productivity	
Machine utilization	Return on net assets
Inventory turnover or	Days of inventory
months on hand	
Cost variances	Product cost, especially relative to competitors' costs
Individual incentives	Group incentives
Performance to schedule	Customer service
Promotion based on	Promotion based on increased knowledge and
seniority	capability
	Ideas generated
	Ideas implemented
	Lead time by product/product family
	Setup reduction
	Number of customer complaints
	Response time to customer feedback
	Machine availability
	Cost of quality

The Spirit of Manufacturing Excellence (Homewood, Ill., 1986).

Specific performance measures are dependent on the unique business environment and the process being managed. For example, Harley Davidson has adopted the following 10 measurements to assess its manufacturing effectiveness:

1. Schedule attainment.
2. Manning requirements.

3. Conservation costs.
4. Overtime requirements (measure of flexibility).
5. Inventory levels.
6. Material cost variance.
7. Scrap/rework.
8. Manufacturing cycle time (measure of flexibility).
9. Quality level.
10. Productivity improvements.

Conversely, a Fortune 100 company has adopted the seven measures and goals listed in Figure 4 for measuring its effectiveness in an integrated circuit facility.

While the measures are different for these two organizations, there are similarities. In both cases, nonfinancial indicators were used to measure performance as part of the cost management system. This is consistent with the identification of true cost drivers outlined earlier and with the focus on quality and lead times.

Both measurement systems were proposed and maintained by the financial executives in these organizations. In each case, the financial executives proposed more effective ways of monitoring performance and reducing overall cost and worked closely with manufacturing to refine these proposals and to establish a "team approach to performance measurement."

Both performance measurement systems were simplified from their predecessor traditional systems. Simple, easy-to-understand measures were implemented so that everyone in the

FIGURE 4

Measure	Goal
1. Unit cost—cell $/hr.—theoretical units/hr.	$1.00
2. Cycle time = through cell with no downtime	3 days
3. On-time delivery	100%
4. Quality	0 defects
5. Linearity—ability to meet daily schedule	0% deviation
6. Inventory turns	75
7. Scrap	0

organization could comprehend the intent and interpret the results of the systems. Additionally, measurement results were posted so that everyone in the organization could be more aware and in tune with company improvements in these areas.

FOCUS ON SIMPLIFICATION

In each of the major areas of cost management outlined previously, specific company solutions differ. The impact of true cost drivers within organizations differs from one company to another; the number of product cost elements necessary to report and control costs properly also differ between companies. The ability to apply costs directly to product and the types of cost being applied to products change based on organizational differences and products being manufactured; and, as has been shown, performance measurements differ between companies.

However, without exception, simplification was one of the primary objectives of every financial executive who enhanced his or her cost management system for JIT. Focus on two or three true cost drivers within an organization, reduction in standard product cost elements, reduction of allocations, and establishment of fewer, easy-to-understand, key performance measures are all examples of simplification.

JIT strives for design and process simplification because with simplification comes better management. Better management allows for better quality, better service, and fewer costs. The same principles are true for cost-management systems. Traditional cost accounting systems tend to be very complex. Simplification of this process enables the cost accounting system to be used by everyone in an organization, transforming the cost "accounting" system into a cost "management" system.

HOW TO INITIATE CHANGE

The management accountant should learn to think "just-in-time accounting." However, he or she must adjust to changing technology, new management philosophies, and the changing informational demands. Nothing is more discouraging than hearing financial people say, "We can't accommodate that change because of our accounting system."

Each organization cited here had successes and failures before focusing on the cost management direction necessary to support JIT. As financial executives related their stories regarding cost management changes, a set of common steps emerged revealing how these changes occurred:

• The perception of the accounting function needed to be changed. In each company the accounting function was perceived as a control function, a function that reported when things were bad. This perception (or reality) had to change from one of control of operations to one of cooperation with operations to reduce costs. The financial executives took the time and effort necessary to understand JIT and joined the operating professionals in an effort to implement it.

• The financial executives became an integral part of the manufacturing and engineering project teams. On a regular basis a cost manager sat in on all product design meetings, manufacturing engineering meetings, and production control and planning meetings. This accomplished the following: (a) accounting personnel learned the key elements of engineering and manufacturing processes; (b) operating personnel became more aware of the implications of their actions on total cost, raising the total cost awareness throughout the company; and (c) perhaps most importantly, executive attendance served as the basis for eliminating communication barriers between accounting and operations. Each objective helped pave the way for obtaining the interfunctional cooperation necessary for the total quality philosophy to work in a company.

• True cost drivers were identified. Once accounting became more aware of operations and operating personnel became more aware of the cost implications of their actions, those processes or engineering issues truly determining cost could be identified, segregated, and attached.

• Each company reanalyzed its application of costs to products and implemented a higher level of direct charging. The elimination of allocations gave a clearer picture of true product costs and raised the responsibility of costs to managers. Again, this is predicated on accounting's understanding of the engineering and production processes.

• Performance measures were altered to help motivate the entire operating group toward positive results. Individual performance measures were reduced to encourage a team concept. Personnel were trained and informed as to the meaning of performance measures.

• All systems were simplified. Traditional accounting systems were redesigned to reflect JIT tenets. Information flows and reports were simplified to focus on critical processes and measures.

Simplification increased awareness and allowed management to focus on only a few issues, greatly increasing the benefits associated with their actions. As process changes took place, cost drivers and performance measurements changed. Financial executives could change reports and information flows to reflect the new manufacturing process quickly and inexpensively.

Virtually any organization can enhance its cost systems to be more supportive of the total quality philosophy. The first step is for the financial executive to adopt the primary total quality principle of continual improvement within the organization and the cost management process.

CHAPTER 14

BUILDING WORLD-CLASS
SUPPLIERS

Steven M. Ray

End the practice of awarding business on the basis of price tag.
Instead, minimize total cost. Move toward a single supplier for
any one item, on a long-term relationship of loyalty and trust
—Dr. W. Edwards Deming

Total cost is not synonymous with price. Despite the fact that
most purchasing professionals are taught to evaluate suppliers
on the basis of price, quality, and service, the costs of quality and
service have remained hidden or ignored. Consequently, initial
price has weighed heavily in procurement decisions. The total
cost of purchased material goes well beyond price. These costs
are outlined here.

1. Quality-related costs:
   a. Incoming inspection.
   b. Vendor returns.
   c. Sorting.
   d. Rework.
   e. Material review board.
   f. Variation.
2. Service-related costs:
   a. Stockouts.
   b. Inventory carrying costs.
3. Opportunity-related costs such as no improvement activity.

A large percentage of quality-related costs are caused by poor specifications. It is the customer's responsibility to ensure that engineering does not arbitrarily determine specifications or add large safety factors to shield them from criticism. Specifications must relate meaningfully to key design characteristics. Meaningful specifications alone, however, will not solve all supplier quality problems. Suppliers must also possess the process capability to meet specifications and strive continually to improve process capability by reducing variation.

Service-related costs are caused by unreliable production systems. Everyone in the supply chain must continuously improve the total production system, reduce wasteful inventory, and enhance flexibility. Quality improvement pertains to everything—not only products and processes.

Opportunity-related costs are caused by misunderstanding and complacency. Adversarial relationships and arm's length dealings do little to improve supplier performance. Supplier performance can be improved and material costs can be reduced by working with a supplier. However, we continue to award business based primarily on price. This results frequently in changes of suppliers, thus never working with one to reduce total costs.

Purchased material costs, as a percentage of sales, are significant and growing. They can be as high as 50–70 percent for many companies. The impact on profitability is obvious. For example, a 10 percent reduction in the total cost of material for a company having material costs of 50 percent of the sales dollar would contribute 5 percent to gross profit. On the surface, this analogy may not appear new, but it is used frequently to point out the importance of managing procurement costs. There is, however, a fundamental difference: the emphasis here is on the reduction of *total* costs.

Because purchase costs are so often equated to price paid, the impetus has been to look constantly for a lower price. Purchasing's job has focused on soliciting quotes and playing suppliers against one another to squeeze out every nickle possible, resulting in frequent changes of suppliers. The fallacy is that while the intent is laudable, manufacturers have actually been increasing total costs.

It is top management's responsibility to change from traditional to enlightened procurement strategies. This responsibility should not be delegated. Purchasing has been doing only what they have been told to do, responding to management's perceived notion of what is important. With the high reliance on purchased material today, achieving manufacturing excellence depends more on developing world-class suppliers than anything else, and top management must lead the way. This chapter addresses the objectives, key elements, and changing roles necessary to develop the supply base into a competitive weapon.

OBJECTIVES

The overriding procurement objective is to build a supplier base committed to the principles and ideals of the quality paradigm, that is, a supplier base continually striving to improve quality, delivery performance, and total costs.

A supplier is an extension of a company's own process, as is the supplier's supplier, and so on through the entire supply chain. The manufacturer's ability to serve its customer, to provide product and service quality, and to create a perception of value is dependent on the ability of the manufacturer's suppliers to serve that manufacturer's needs.

Improving Delivery Performance

Improving delivery performance relates not only to on-time delivery, but also to more frequent manufacture and delivery of smaller quantities. Since inventory is a waste and a hindrance to flexibility, the answer is not to push inventory back to suppliers. Regardless of who stores it, the inventory still exists, thereby impeding progress. Suppliers must improve their production systems' reliability. In fact, all manufacturers in the supply chain must continually strive to improve productivity, quality, customer service, and flexibility.

Improving Total Cost

Studies have shown that because the cost of quality averages 20–30 percent of total sales dollars, the most important element in improving total cost is improving quality. In addition to understanding the various techniques used to achieve cost reduction, it is important to understand first where the opportunities are. After establishing new relationships built on trust, customers and suppliers must learn to work together to identify and prioritize those opportunities, to establish plans, and to set targets for improvement.

Synergism

Each manufacturer working alone in a supply chain will always be constrained by the quality received from its suppliers. The quality of incoming materials also greatly influences the quality of products sold to the next customer in the chain. However, all manufacturers, working together to understand better one another's needs and to improve one another's capabilities, eventually will benefit. Customers must assist suppliers under a new working relationship governed by shared values and mutual trust. In turn, suppliers must possess the knowledge and skill to capitalize on the newfound relationship and to extend the principles of excellence to their suppliers. The resulting synergism is essential to a sustained U.S. presence in today's world market.

KEY ELEMENTS

Building a world-class supplier base is not an easy task. The following key elements should be considered when developing new procurement strategies.

Get Your Own House in Order First

If you do not possess the requisite knowledge and skill to improve your own quality and the reliability of your own production systems, there is little you can do to assist your suppliers. The risk of doing something is that it could result in tampering and perhaps make things worse. Supplier development is not the place to start on the journey toward manufacturing excellence. Manufacturers must first invest heavily in developing internal capability. Furthermore, even given a thorough understanding of these concepts and ideals, persuading suppliers to change without you yourself having successfully applied that knowledge and skill will be difficult. Once applied, however, selling the concepts will come easily since it is difficult to argue with success.

Reduced Supplier Base

For the buyer, reducing the supplier base is essential to improvement for three primary reasons: reduced variation, increased supplier commitment, and efficient use of internal resources.

Reduced Variation

Even though two manufacturers can manufacture and ship product that meets specifications, there will always be differences. One product may display greater variation in dimensions or other characteristics, yet still fall within specification. Or one may be centered on different values within the specification, resulting in greater combined variation for the two products, although total variation for each product is the same. (see Figure 1). These differences impact your process and the ultimate performance of the end product. Adding a third supplier further compounds the problem. For this reason, no individual part should be sourced by more than a single supplier.

Supplier Commitment

By consolidating purchases with a single supplier under a long-term relationship, more is at stake for both customer and supplier. Greater volumes and economies beget greater commitment from the supplier to satisfy customer needs. And suppliers

FIGURE 1
Effect of Multiple Suppliers on Variation

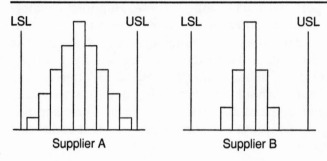

In the above case, both suppliers meet specifications.
However, supplier A's product has more variation.

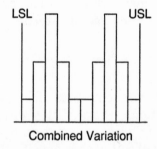

Combined Variation

In this case, both suppliers have about the same variation,
but centered around different values. The combined effect
is again more variation.

are willing to invest in improvement once the fear of losing the
business due to lower prices is removed.

Internal Resources

Building a world-class supplier base demands investment of
time and other resources to develop and maintain supplier
relations and to work jointly to improve quality, delivery, and
cost. Few manufacturers have the resources to work effectively

with multiple suppliers of each part. Instead, buyers should strive to source multiple parts with a given supplier to conserve resources, to strengthen commitment, and to enhance the effectiveness of customer-supplier relations.

Supplier Selection

Traditionally, suppliers have been evaluated on price. Even though consideration may be given to areas such as financial strength, technical capacity, and on-time delivery performance, it is usually an act of ratification or corroboration of a decision based primarily on price, rather than on a thorough evaluation of supplier worthiness.

To build a world-class supplier base, suppliers must be carefully selected based on the following:

- *Capability* to improve quality, delivery, and cost.
- *Willingness* to commit to becoming world class.

New evidence to support the notion that a prospective supplier is both capable and willing to become world class is needed to ensure proper evaluation of suppliers. Following is a partial list of questions to ask. The criteria for the Malcolm Baldrige National Quality Award[1] also provide an excellent architecture for a comprehensive supplier assessment and are highly recommended.

1. Corporate leadership:
   a. Does the corporate mission statement emphasize commitment to excellence?

---

[1]For a list of the Malcolm Baldrige criteria, write or call the following:
The Malcolm Baldrige National Quality Award Consortium, Inc.
P.O. Box 443
Milwaukee, Wisconsin 53201–0443
Telephone (414) 272–8575

P.O. Box 56606, Dept. 698
Houston, Texas 77256–6606
Telephone (713) 681–4020

    b. Is there a corporatewide quality improvement plan? goals? What progress has been made?

    c. Are corporate policies consistent with a commitment to excellence?

    d. What is the role of top management in quality improvement? To what degree are they involved?

    e. Are quality audits performed? How often? What is the substance of the audits?

    f. What resources are allocated to quality improvement? What education and training? What staff? What funds? What equipment?

2. Customer focus:

    a. Does the company measure customer satisfaction? How? What is it?

    b. How are customer needs assessed? satisfied?

3. Analytical tools and techniques:

    a. To what extent does the company understand and use cost of quality measures; quality function deployment; design of experiments; or statistical process control?

4. Employee involvement:

    a. To what extent are employees involved in improvement efforts? Who is involved? At what levels are employees involved? How much time is spent?

    b. What education and training is provided? Are quality, JIT, and employee involvement concepts used? Are team dynamics, problem solving, and analytical tools and techniques employed?

5. Just-in-time:

    a. To what degree have inventories and cycle times been reduced?

    b. How reliable is tooling and equipment? To what degree is total productive maintenance employed?

    c. What progress has been made in reducing setup time?

    d. Have employees been empowered to shut down the process when problems are encountered?

    e. What progress has been made toward cellular manufacturing and pull production?

6. Financial strength:
    a. What is the corporate profit history?
    b. What is the corporate ROI?
    c. What are the corporate debt/equity and other ratios?
7. Design and technical ability:
    a. Does the company have a history of technological innovation?
    b. What funds are allocated to R & D?
    c. What is the design cycle time? Are there plans to reduce it? What are they? What progress has been made?
    d. What is being done to design for manufacturability?
8. Trends in key performance indicators:
    a. Cost of quality? External failure? Internal failure? Appraisal? Prevention?
    b. Costs?
    c. Cycle time?
    d. On-time delivery performance?

Asking the correct questions and requiring supporting evidence are crucial steps toward building a world-class supplier base. Once the supplier base has been reduced and includes only the best available choices, an investment must be made in building new relationships.

New Relationships

Selecting the correct suppliers is a crucial, yet only a beginning, step. Traditionally, purchasing has dealt with suppliers at arm's length. Relationships have been adversarial and built on mutual distrust. Suppliers have been played against each other in hopes of attaining lower prices. Consequently, suppliers have been unwilling to invest in the relationship and to improve products and services for fear of losing their investment along with the business. Even if suppliers were willing to invest in the relationship, customers have been reluctant to share ideas, information, technology, and details of processes for fear of them being using against them, making it difficult (if not impossible) for suppliers to assist their customers and make improvements. In this sense, relationships have been closed.

Building a world-class supplier base demands the formation and cultivation of new relationships based on mutual respect, cooperation, and trust. Both customer and supplier must make a long-term commitment because it is the only way to ensure that improvement initiatives will be fruitful. Continuous improvement is a long-term, never-ending process, and to change suppliers after having made gains is akin to starting over.

Ken Stork of Motorola believes that "the customer must be proactive in breaking down adversarial relationships that have existed for decades. To help do this, our Communications sector established a Partnership Growth Advisory Board. This board includes 15 supplier executives who repeatedly are encouraged to advise Motorola about what it needs to improve to become a world-class company from their perspective."

Customers and suppliers must cooperate and be willing to share information and technology once considered sensitive. Involving suppliers in product design will add technical expertise, help ensure manufacturability, and cut design cycle times. Studying one another's processes fosters understanding of mutual needs and capabilities, leading to better focus and decision making in improvement activities. Transferring ideas in the long term benefits both.

Communications must be open and direct because purchasing can no longer funnel all communications. The volume and substance of these communications must increase dramatically. Funneling the communications through the buyer will only distort the message, as in the "telephone" party game. Besides, no buyer possesses the technical skills required to have meaningful discussions on all issues. Customers and suppliers must establish direct communications between technical experts— quality engineer to quality engineer, design engineer to design engineer, production planner to production planner, and so forth.

The role of purchasing becomes one of managing the relationship. All purchasers must be aware of joint efforts and communications in order to facilitate improvement. This is a dramatic departure from the traditional purchaser role and an immense personal and cultural change that cannot be treated lightly.

Working Partnership

Once the supplier base has been reduced and new relationships formed, customer and supplier must work together as partners. Formal meetings should be held on a quarterly or semiannual basis to exchange information and to plan for the future. The following are some issues that need to be addressed:

- Business projections.
- Mutual needs, concerns, and expectations of the relationship.
- Education and training needs.
- Design projects requiring joint efforts.
- R & D efforts and technological developments.
- Cost reduction opportunities.
- Joint strategies, plans, and goals for improvement.

Exchanges should occur both at top management and operational levels. Top management should spend as much time with critical suppliers as with their customers to strengthen the supply chain and to improve their product and service quality.

On a day-to-day basis, open and direct communication between customer and supplier technical experts should occur naturally as needed to accomplish objectives. Purchasing's role is to facilitate these changes and exchanges, to monitor progress toward agreed-upon goals and objectives, and to ensure that issues impeding progress are addressed. Purchasing should encourage and participate in formal exchanges and planning efforts. They should also ensure that suppliers receive adequate feedback in terms of agreed-upon targets, should facilitate quick responses to day-to-day operating problems, and should bring the correct parties together to solve these problems.

Education, Training, and Technical Assistance

Unfortunately, in the search for ideal suppliers few have the capabilities needed. Therefore, customers must be prepared to provide education, training, and technical assistance. Ford, Motorola, and Xerox have exerted considerable energy to educate their suppliers (even though their competitors buy from the same supplier). This assistance can take many forms, including the following:

- Recommending sources for education, training, and technical assistance.
- Sponsoring or conducting in-house education and training sessions.
- Providing hands-on technical assistance at the supplier's plant.
- Demonstrating the application of various tools and techniques at the customer's plant.

Learning is enhanced greatly when people can apply new knowledge and skill immediately. Joint efforts to resolve problems, to make improvements, or to recommend outside consulting services are all valuable means for developing needed skills.

Measurements

Building a world-class supplier base demands significant cultural and behavioral changes at all company levels. Often overlooked is the need to change existing measurement systems to motivate new behaviors. Management must thoroughly assess current measurements, eliminating those that motivate old behaviors, while developing new measures to motivate desired behaviors. Ignoring this issue will only create conflict and confusion. For example, if purchasing is asked to stop awarding business on a price basis alone, although purchasers are still measured on purchase-price variance or price-reduction targets, all will continue to look at price.

Aggregate or composite measures are better than detailed measures. These evaluations should be performed over longer periods of time while looking for trends in many data points. As with anything else, measures are subject to random variation. Highly detailed measures and judgments based on the movement of only a few data points can result in tampering and mistakes. Therefore, emphasis should be placed on improvement in quality, on-time delivery, delivery frequency, and total cost reduction.

Recognize that purchasing alone cannot be held responsible for improvement. Many functions at all levels must contribute to supplier development. It is best for management to lead and to be involved in supplier-improvement initiatives, knowing firsthand what effort is being spent and the progress made. Involvement is better than trying to second-guess performance by looking at some arbitrary or capricious numbers. Management by historical numbers is akin to walking backwards: it is difficult to stay on course and to judge distance.

THE BUYER'S ROLE

It is human nature to resist change, often unknowingly. The approach to building world-class suppliers involves a significant departure from traditional methods of managing the supplier base and an immense personal and professional change for buyers. Buyers must

- Acquire the requisite knowledge.
- Select only the best suppliers for the long term. End the practice of awarding business only on a price basis. Work with others to evaluate suppliers based on capability and willingness to become world class.
- Focus on improving supplier quality, delivery performance, and total cost. Understand the relationship between quality and cost.
- Manage supplier relationships. Facilitate change and exchange. End the practice of funneling communications by promoting open and direct communications. Take the lead in planning and establishing improvement goals.
- Monitor progress and assist in removing any barriers to an effective working partnership.

CONCLUSION

Manufacturing companies cannot become world class alone. Their entire supplier community must become world class, also. Given the strong tradition of adversarial relationships between buyers and sellers, evolving to long-term cooperative arrangements with sole-source suppliers is a profound cultural change. Only top management can set the tone to effect this change.

CHAPTER 15

QUALITY IMPROVEMENT AND AUTOMATION

William Duncan
Rich Hammond
Ernest C. Huge
Ron Roman
Gerald Vasily

Today the secret of building world-class manufacturing and service capabilities lies in making numerous investments over a long period of time—small investments, as well as large investments. The total quality culture described in this book can ensure that these numerous investments are the correct ones and ensure that the firm is ready to make full productive use of them when acquired. The traditional capital budgeting process must be replaced by a more proactive, multilevel, interdisciplinary approach toward resource allocation. Here, as elsewhere, total quality has great impact on a firm's planning and competitiveness.

In *The Spirit of Manufacturing Excellence,* different strategies for implementing automation technology in manufacturing are analyzed. Automation includes computer-integrated technology in engineering and manufacturing. Many companies that invested heavily in these technologies often have experienced disappointment regarding gains in productivity and quality. This is because their company's quality cultures were not ready to implement the new technology.

To implement these systems successfully, a firm's environment must first attain a high degree of discipline vis-à-vis total quality. In fact, many benefits sought through automation are attainable simply by developing the total quality process and its techniques and forgoing new automation. As total quality becomes more enmeshed in the company's know-how, procuring automation may make sense.

Automation has been defined as "The application of fully automatic procedures in the efficient performance and control of a sequence of standardized and repetitive processes." Automation's definition has expanded somewhat since it was listed this way in the early 1970s. With the advent of computerization and widespread efforts to integrate this technology into every aspect of the manufacturing business, automation has come to mean a great many things to many different disciplines. Most recently, these efforts have been encompassed by the terms *computer-integrated manufacturing (CIM)* or *computer integrated enterprise*. According to Teicholz and Orr in *The Computer Integrated Manufacturing (CIM) Handbook,* computer-integrated manufacturing has come to describe "the complete automation of the factory, with all processes functioning under computer control and only digital information tying them together. In CIM, the need for paper is eliminated, and so also are most human jobs."

What, then, are these new technologies? Among them are the following:

Group technology (GT)—A system centered on families of parts, with families organized by virtue of similarities in materials and dimensional characteristics. Group technology allows more rapid and efficient design, promotes standardization, and facilitates computer-aided manufacturing (CAM).

Computer-aided design (CAD) or computer-aided engineering (CAE)—A system that allows drafting, modeling, finite-element analysis, and actual design work to be done on a computer, rather than on a drafting board. The design information is digitized, and thereby available for maintenance, communication, and translation into hard copy anywhere digital data can be moved.

Computer-aided process planning (CAPP)—A system comprising part descriptions, manufacturing process information, and tooling data. The purpose of CAPP is to store and apply process data to gain efficiencies in the development of the manufacturing process for individual parts/assemblies. *Numerical control* (NC)—A system involving the control of a machine or process by means of directly fed symbolic and numerical values. Numerical control systems typically involve many types of numerically controlled devices, including numerically controlled machines/machine groups, robotics, automated guided vehicles (AGVs), and other programmable devices, CNC refers to computer numerically controlled equipment.

Cost justification is an obstacle that is often difficult for any new manufacturing approach to overcome. To quote William Muir from the *CIM Handbook,* "The implication of state-of-the-art manufacturing processes in a typical U.S. manufacturing company will not, in and of itself, improve productivity or reduce costs." There are a number of messages implicitly stated here, not the least of which is that no system or approach can be casually selected or haphazardly applied with any realistic expectation of success.

Estimating the likely improvement from these applications requires more than traditional capital justification activities. Especially in automation approaches, where capital investments are usually high and technology is becoming passé at a frightening pace, the justification process can become extremely complex. These processes normally involve the development of a detailed cost model, considering amortization of the proposed equipment and facilities, utilization, support costs (particularly information management), and personnel requirements. In either the automation of simplification scenario, it is necessary to estimate efficiencies that may be gained in the areas of labor (direct, indirect, and administrative), inventory (raw materials, work-in-process, finished goods), throughput times, and quality levels (reduced scrap, rework, warranty claims). However, there are other new strategic issues that senior management must address in its capital budgeting process. Here total quality planning can help greatly.

The media have focused on highly automated plants, such as GM's Saturn or the Hamtramch plant in Michigan. Hamtramch is a $600 million assembly plant designed to be a showcase for automated high technology. The plant has 260 robots for assembly and painting, 50 automated guided vehicles to ferry parts, and a battery of cameras and computers using laser beams to inspect and control the manufacturing process. Unfortunately, Hamtramch is turning out only 30 cars an hour, although it is designed to produce 60 an hour. Japanese firms use automation, though in smaller doses. A new Mazda Motors plant in Michigan costs 25 percent less to operate than Hamtramch because it lacks most of GM's sophisticated automation. Yet the plant is producing 240,000 cars a year with 3,500 workers, while Hamtramch has 5,000 workers and aims at only 220,000 cars a year when everything works as it should.

The lesson is that with just the right amount of technology, lower investment and higher productivity result. To know what "just the right amount" of technology is requires a strategic understanding fostered first by implementing the total quality basics. Automation can cut costs and increase quality in the long run and provide so much product flexibility that industry may resemble a manufacturing boutique. Yet this is feasible only if the spirit of total quality takes hold. Only then can a firm start making the continuing series of large and small allocation decisions that singularly and synergistically produce a world-class competitor.

Such decisions require the participation and input of employees from all levels and most disciplines. They require everyone to share a common vision and understanding of a firm's values, objectives, and strategies. In other words, policy deployment is needed. Only then can all employees make, day by day or hour by hour, decisions that are harmonious with the firm's general mission, and that will advance the firm's position in its business environment.

If decisions are made without a shared guiding vision or strategy, the company will most likely be inefficient and at cross-purposes. Today major decisions are made by senior managers aware of the firm's mission, but it is not solely these major projects that are strategically critical. Competitors are channeling the strategic impact of thousands of other decisions too small to warrant most U.S. senior managers' attentions. Typically, these have been handled through a variety of systems, procedures, and ingrained behavior patterns—the managerial infrastructure. If these systems are faulty, even though senior management decisions are made with care and purpose, the resultant structure may not be competitive. Yet, if this infrastructure has been developed using policy deployment and the total quality paradigm, it will continually advance the firm competitively.

The capital investment process, by its nature, has encouraged in companies a preference for big projects—the kind requiring preparation of a capital authorization request (CAR) and subject to detailed analyses—over small projects. However, the secret to building world-class manufacturing capabilities often lies in making numerous little investments over a long period of time. Such investments tend to bubble up in entrepreneurial fashion from lower levels in the organization. Neither senior management nor their corporate staffs are likely to get involved in such projects. In fact, most of them are almost invisible above the factory level because they are paid for out of operating budgets. This lack of visibility—together with their reliance on the personal, subjective, judgment of lower-level managers rather than on the objective, rational analysis applied to formal CAR—causes many top managers to regard them with suspicion.

Too many companies focus on major investments, such as buying an existing off-the-shelf system rather than using in-house capabilities, to design and implement customized processes, one by one, "brick by brick," over a long period of time. These companies focus too much attention on the investment rather than on the long-term implications of that investment.

Something of the old New England model of Yankee ingenuity, where owners and partners rubbed elbows with skilled crafters and workers, should be kept in mind. Owners knew the shop floor and were keyed into any new ideas or ways of making the business better. This "Yankee school" of economics reminds us that the accumulated impact of attention to smaller details can make a company exceptional.

In Chapter Six of *The Spirit of Manufacturing Excellence,* these contrasting approaches were called the "grinding it out" and the "going for the long bomb" approaches to automation (see Figure 1).

"Grinding it out" is the slower, more-effective way to capture the advantage of new technologies and is in tune with total quality. It entails mastering the elements of total quality to derive the most from existing equipment and to educate employees in the new cultural infrastructure of cooperation and participation. Only then is further automation considered, and, when appropriate, automation is integrated. One key intermediate step is what Toyota calls *autonomation,* which means that equipment detecting problems stops automatically when necessary. A further step involves automated self-correction. Here improving the process by internal capability is emphasized. In-house personnel adapt equipment to the needs of the specific process. As a result, the adapted equipment cannot be purchased externally. It becomes a proprietary process and, as such, a competitive advantage. This approach requires much time and that many small steps be taken every day. Figure 2 reflects the degree of automating manufacturing cells.

"Going for the long bomb" means simplifying, automating, and integrating simultaneously. Instead of custom designing

FIGURE 1
Comparison of Strategic Approaches

Criteria	"Grinding It Out"	"Going for the Long Bomb"
Complexity and cost	Less	More
Ease of implementation	Easier	Harder
Break-even volume	Lower	Higher
Risk	Less	More
Relative benefits	Possibly less initially	Possibly more sooner
Appropriation by the competition	Difficult	Easier

FIGURE 2
Degree of Automating Manufacturing Cells

	I	II	III Flexible Machining Cell (FMC)	IV (FMS) Flexible Machining Systems
Machine tools	Conventional	Conventional and NC/CNC	NC/CNC only	CNC only
Material handling	Manual	Manual	Manual	Automated
Quality assurance	Manual	Manual	Autonomation	Automated corrective action
Overall control of the cell	Manual	Manual	Manual	Computer

processes, the firm purchases off-the-shelf equipment. The focus is on integrating general-purpose equipment and using the flexible machining systems (FMS). Off-the-shelf technology does not give a sustainable competitive advantage because everyone can buy it. Also, general off-the-shelf processes are more expensive than custom-designed processes. These processes are general in application and must accommodate many different situations; therefore, they are not as efficient as a process specifically designed for a given situation. Both strategies can work, but "grinding it out" is more desirable because it ensures that inefficiencies are not automated and that benefits from implementing the basic quality tools are not used to justify high-cost automation.

JUSTIFICATION OF TECHNOLOGY

Traditionally, new technology and its required capital investments have been justified by its return on investment (ROI) and its reduction of labor calculations. Unfortunately, this approach to acquisition of new technology does not factor into the strategic impact of these decisions. Today, many new technologies have a significant impact on such important considerations as the quality of products, delivery speed and reliability, and the rapidity with which new products can be designed, manufactured, and introduced. Examples of such computer-assisted manufacturing technologies are computer-aided-design/computer-aided manufacturing (CAD/CAM), flexible manufacturing systems (FMS), and computer-integrated manufacturing (CIM). Many U.S. companies do not understand the capabilities of these new technologies and the strategic impact they may have on an organization.

Therefore, some new automation technologies are so fundamentally different that they have the potential to change the way manufacturing, engineering, and marketing organizations interact and how the company as a whole interacts with its customers. The strategic dimensions of this new technology need to be understood and incorporated to justify its acquisition. The corporate infrastructure arising from total quality (through employee involvement, policy deployment, quality function deployment, etc.) makes informed and enlightened investment decisions possible throughout the firm.

Another consideration that justifies the new technologies is the strategic and economic synergies that often arise when several, or all, are in place. Typically, to justify an investment, each technology project is analyzed separately. Individually, however, a project may not meet corporate profitability criteria. The interdependencies that may exist between a group technology system, a computer-aided-design system, or a customer communication system are not readily included in the traditional capital budgeting process.

Yet another automation aspect not easily included in financial justification analyses is that many resemble research and development projects as much as they do standard capital investments. Automation can create new knowledge and new capabilities, as well as facilitate significant learning. However, the degree of interaction with other projects and the nature of the risks incurred are almost impossible to estimate in advance. So, too, are the profitable opportunities that may be uncovered in the future as a result of making the investment now. Here again a more sensitive reading is needed to assess this new technology's potential.

Justification of new technology must not only generate and shape decisions so that they achieve a required level of financial attractiveness, but it must also spotlight and facilitate investments to build and sustain some type of competitive advantage. It should seek to create the future the company desires. Otherwise, justification of new technology may back investments that do not support the firm's vision of the future.

Dynamic Manufacturing by Robert Hayes, Steven Wheelwright, and Kim Clark suggests that the traditional justification process be placed in a broader framework to include the preceding considerations. This larger framework incorporates an understanding of competitive factors and requires that investments yield an acceptable financial return and improve the firm's competitive position. Financial evaluation should be linked to customer behavior research, to research on the firm's organizational capabilities, and to the overall business plan. An understanding of customers reveals how an investment creates value. An understanding of the new capabilities of an investment reveals the competitive advantage it offers.

Dynamic Manufacturing also outlines how to analyze the ways a capital investment can create a competitive advantage. The authors outline a three-step approach that determines first, how an investment affects the company's products and capabilities, and second, how the investments impact the firm's commercial and technical capabilities. Working through a product profile analysis and the investments' implications for capability development provides insight into how it will create value, what must be done to manage its implementation, and how difficult it will be for competitors to acquire similar capabilities.

The third step determines how to integrate these insights into a general assessment of the investment's attractiveness. This requires an understanding of the interaction between the technical and commercial domains, as well as between the firm's capabilities and its customers. Furthermore, what the investment means to a firm's financial health must be clarified in order to generate insight into the financial implications of alternative courses of action. Finally, it is necessary to scrutinize how a proposed investment meshes with the business's strategy and the business's functional areas. This last step goes a long way toward establishing a common perspective of an investment's purpose because it requires marketing, sales, manufacturing, R & D, and finance to communicate with one another and to develop a shared vision of the investment vis-à-vis their firm's mission. Without this total quality infrastructure, justifying investments in new technology may continue to disappoint U.S. firms.

CONCLUSION

INSPIRING LEADERSHIP: PEOPLE FIRST

Ernest C. Huge
Gerald Vasily

People are the heart and spirit of all that counts. This is the fundamental value underlying our Judeo-Christian civilization. It is also the fundamental value and ethic of companies renown for their excellence. As W. Edwards Deming writes, we are in a new economic age with an abundant supply of quality goods and with managements playing by new rules. These rules are the complex infrastructure of new values, beliefs, policies, and relationships described in this book—and they all flow from putting people first. All of these rules, foremost the value of the person, need to be more broadly implanted in our own capitalistic economic system to ensure their continued vitality.

Capitalism, the best economic system yet developed, possesses unfortunate shortcomings of being too exclusive. Unemployment and the employee's objectification as a commodity of labor have excluded many from both capitalism's process and a generally equitable distribution of its results. In 1947, General MacArthur mandated that Japanese industry provide for full employment in its economic system. As a result, the Japanese had to develop systems and processes that allowed their nation to prosper within this mandate. Ironically, these same policies and systems designed to allow for full employment have given the Japanese the competitive advantage.

To maintain full employment in a period of rapid technological change, companies have had to invest heavily in training and education to keep employees highly productive. Also, compensation has been structured to keep everyone employed throughout the business cycle. In Japan, compensation can be 30–50 percent profit sharing. In a good year, everyone is rewarded; in a lean year, everyone is working. Now, in the 1990s, Western automakers are following suit by putting a greater percentage of their employees' compensation into profit sharing. This approach is eminently sensible given the enormous costs of training.

Leaders of top Japanese companies exhibit a trustee mentality to a greater degree than U.S. management. They feel they have been entrusted with the responsibility to create and sustain an environment that supports numerous individuals. Such a leader is more aware of the customers, families, suppliers, and community that his or her decisions impact. Abraham Lincoln was such a leader, as demonstrated by his passionate, personal concern to preserve the American Union.

Like everyone else, the Japanese can be egotistical, prideful, and greedy. It is not necessary to totally eliminate these characteristics, only to exhibit them less frequently than the competition. Obviously, the Japanese have been successful in achieving this: they have manifested the values of trusteeship in business better than U.S. business has, and this has given them the critical edge.

The great Japanese companies view work as an integral part of a person's life. They believe people are idealistic. American business must also believe this, for there is a tremendous human need to work toward ideals. All too often this remains a great untapped resource throughout a company because all of us have a need to serve and to make a difference.

In the United States, the issue is much more than economic. Until now, most people, including many managers, have never enjoyed being a significant part of the work environment. Happily, business has continued to shift from a practice of management through formal organizational power to a process of leadership through cooperation and participation.

The primary prerequisites for being an effective leader are to be clear about one's fundamental beliefs about human nature and to be certain of the role of the organization. Managers, especially, need a grounding belief to inform their vision of the person. For many of us, much study and centuries of reflection have uncovered no better ideal than the Christian image of humanity. This philosophy states that humanity is good, is gifted, and has a deep-seated desire to contribute.

To embrace this vision, a leader must appreciate the unique gifts, talents, and skills of every employee. When a manager accepts and appreciates the unique giftedness of every person, whether mechanic or marketer, it becomes clear that each of us is needed. For participative management, it supplies the strength for all of us, whether manager or employee, to think about being abandoned to the gifts and talents of others.

This viewpoint considers a janitor's work, when carried out in the spirit of service, cooperation, and community, to be as noble as that of a senior manager. The values of order, cleanliness, diligence, and meticulousness are proclaimed by a janitor who approaches his or her job as a professional.

The simple act of recognizing the diversity of talent in our business relationships helps a manager connect and activate people's various abilities to the task of the corporation. Max DePree, CEO of Herman Miller, in *Leadership Is an Art,* suggests we think of the leader, in the words of the gospel writer Luke, as "one who serves." The paradoxical psychology behind leader as servant is proven best by our own lives and experiences. How many of us have made our career commitments because a supervisor or professor went out of his or her way to shepherd us along? In return, we respond with generosity. Leadership is a way of thinking about management more as a trusteeship or stewardship than as an ownership.

A good leader sees all persons' abilities and aids them in realizing their full potentials. To a great extent, this means helping them complete their jobs effectively and in a life-enhancing way. The best leader cares enough to listen. He or she listens to the ideas, needs, aspirations, and wishes of all employees, then responds appropriately according to a thoroughly defined value system. The best leader cares enough to explain *why*, not just what.

Beliefs and values, by necessity, precede policy and practice. Our values and personal philosophy also display an integrity with our working lives, just as they do with our families and our social lives. Too often there is a tremendous gap between how we see ourselves as persons and how we see ourselves as workers. A greater sense of integrity and continuity needs to replace this gap. Our sense of self-worth and identity is greatly defined by our work. At its best, work should be productive, fulfilling, and joyful.

Our founding fathers placed the angel of freedom high atop the dome of Washington's Capitol Building. Perhaps little replicas of her should be given to each aspiring leader, since the gift of freedom, more than anything else, enables us to exercise our gifts. We must give each other the space to grow, to be ourselves, to aspire. In this way leaders and their people form a covenant that goes beyond the employment contract, quid-pro-quos, and labor arbitration. Only a leader who genuinely respects employees can give this gift of freedom. Out of this gift comes many things—shared commitment to values, ideas, goals, issues, and management processes. For many, out of this comes some sense of the sacredness of what we are about in our work.

We realize the monkey is on your back to achieve short-term results. However, what is outlined here, more than anything else, is required for your competitive survival. We challenge you to exercise the tremendous courage it requires to implement this vision. To all of you who have started to "walk the talk" we extend our sincerest compliments and wishes for continued success. The spirit behind the process of total quality will see you through with Godspeed.

APPENDIX

RUN CHARTS

A. *Definitions*
  1. A *run chart* plots data over time (see Figure 1).
  2. The *median* is the middle value if the data points are ordered from low to high.
     Note: If there is an even number of values, the median is the average of the two middle values.
  3. A *run about the median* is comprised of consecutive data points above or below the median.
     For example, there are five runs in Figure 2.
     Note: When not referenced to the median, runs relate to consecutive points that meet certain conditions as described next.
B. *Interpreting Run Charts*
  A run chart displays evidence of *special cause* if any of the following conditions exist:
  Conditions
  1. Too many runs or not enough runs about the median for a given number of data points (Figures 3 and 4).

FIGURE 1

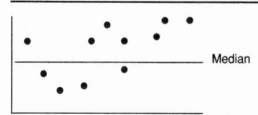

Time   For the data 3, 8, 11, 12, 14, the median is 11

FIGURE 2

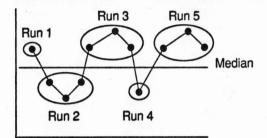

In the data 2, 5, 7, 11, 18, 26, the middle values are 7 and 11 and the median is $(7 + 11)/2 = 9$.

FIGURE 3

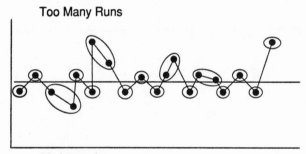

Too Many Runs

20 data points
16 runs

FIGURE 4

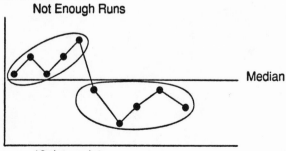

Not Enough Runs

10 data points
2 runs

Number of Data Points	Lower Limit (Not enough runs if less than this number)	Upper Limit (Too many runs if greater than this number)
10	3	8
15	4	12
20	6	15
25	9	17
30	11	20
35	13	23
40	15	26
45	17	29
50	19	32

2. Seven consecutive points that are increasing or decreasing (Figure 5).
3. Eight or more consecutive points on the same side of the median (Figure 6).

FIGURE 5

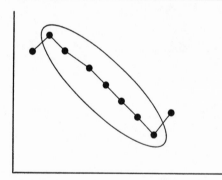

FIGURE 6

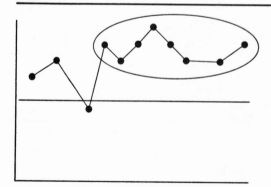

4. Fourteen or more consecutive points alternating up and down (Figure 7).
5. Seven or more consecutive points having the same value (Figure 8).

Notes:
1. When counting runs around the median, omit points on the median.
2. When counting runs up and down, omit points that repeat the previous value.

Sources:
1. Duncan, A. J. *Quality Control and Industrial Statistics.*
2. AT&T. *Western Electric Handbook.*
3. Ford Motor Company. *Continuing Improvement and Process Control.*

FIGURE 7

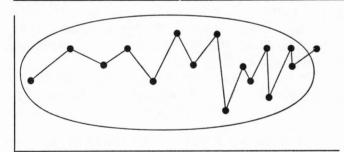

FIGURE 8

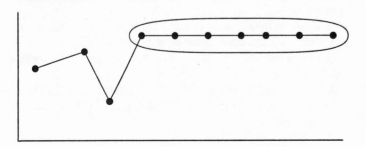

BIBLIOGRAPHY

Abegglen, James C., and George Stalk, Jr. *Kaisha, The Japanese Corporation.* New York: Basic Books, Inc., 1985.

Ashburn, Thomas. "Hoshin Kanri, The Orchestration of Continuous Improvement." Presented at the Fifth Annual GOAL/QPC Conference, Plymouth, Mass., 1988.

Barker, Thomas B. "Quality Engineering by Design: Taguchi's Philosophy." *Quality Progress,* December 1986, pp. 32–42.

Bennis, Warren, and Burt Nanus. *Leaders.* New York: Harper & Row, 1985.

Bhote, Keki R. *Supplier Management.* New York: American Management Association, 1987.

The Bible, King James Version. Wheaton, Ill.: Tyndale House, 1981.

Block, Peter. *The Empowered Manager: Positive Political Skills at Work.* San Francisco: Jossey-Bass, 1988.

Box, George E. P. *Journal of Quality Technology* 17 no. 4, pp. 189–90.

Brassard, Michael. "Key Points in Management by Planning." Presented at the Fifth Annual GOAL/QPC Conference, Plymouth, Mass., 1988.

Buzzell, Robert D., and Bradley T. Gale. *The PIMS Principles.* New York: Free Press, 1987.

Crosby, Philip B. *Quality Is Free.* New York: McGraw-Hill, 1979.

Deming, W. Edwards. *Out of the Crisis.* Cambridge, Mass.: MIT Center for Advanced Engineering Study, 1986.

DePree, Max. *Leadership Is an Art.* East Lansing, Mich.: Michigan State University Press, 1987.

Duncan, William L. *Just-in-Time in American Manufacturing.* Dearborn, Mich.: Society of Manufacturing Engineers, 1988.

Ealey, Lance. "QFD—Bad Name for a Great System." *Automotive Industries,* July 1987, p. 21.

Garvin, David A. *Managing Quality.* New York: Free Press, 1988.

Gleason Components Group, *Global Manufacturing and Us,* Rochester, New York: Summer 1988.

Gunter, Berton. "A Perspective on the Taguchi Methods." *Quality Progress,* June 1987, pp. 44–52.

Hall, Robert W. *Attaining Manufacturing Excellence.* Homewood, Ill.: Dow Jones-Irwin, 1987.

Harrington, H. James. *The Improvement Process: How America's Leading Companies Improve Quality.* New York: McGraw-Hill, 1987.

Hayes, Robert H., Steven C. Wheelwright, and Kim B. Clark. *Dynamic Manufacturing.* New York: Free Press, 1988.

Huge, Ernest C. *The Spirit of Manufacturing Excellence.* Homewood, Ill.: Dow Jones-Irwin, 1987.

Imai, Masaaki. *Kaizen: The Key to Japan's Competitive Success.* New York: Random House, 1986.

Ishikawa, Kaoru. *Guide to Quality Control.* Tokyo: Asian Productivity Organization, 1982. U.S. Distributor: UNIPUB, New York.

———. *What is Total Quality Control?: The Japanese Way.* Englewood Cliffs, N.J.: Prentice-Hall, 1985.

Japan Management Association. *Canon Production System.* Cambridge: Productivity Press, 1987.

Jessup, Peter T. "The Value of Continuing Improvements." *Proceedings of the International Communications Conference, ICC 1985,* Institute of Electrical and Electronics Engineers, June 1985.

Juran, Joseph M. *Juran on Leadership for Quality.* New York: Free Press, 1989.

Kackar, Raghu N. "Off-Line Quality Control, Parameter, Design and the Taguchi Method." *Journal of Quality Technology* 17 no. 4, pp. 176–88.

———. "Taguchi's Quality Philosophy: Analysis and Commentary. *Quality Progress,* December 1986, pp. 21–29.

Kogure, Masao, and Akao, Yoji. "Quality Function Deployment and CWQC in Japan." *Quality Progress,* October 1983, pp. 25–29.

Maccoby, Michael. *Why Work.* New York: Simon and Schuster, 1988.

Mizuno, Shigeru. *Company-Wide Total Quality Control.* Tokyo: Asian Productivity Organization, 1988.

Morita, Akio. *Made in Japan.* New York: Dutton, 1986.

Nakajima, Sciichi. *Total Productive Maintenance.* Cambridge, Mass.: Productivity Press, 1988.

Nora, John, C., Raymond Rogers, and Robert Stanny. *Transforming the Workplace.* Princeton, N.J.: Princeton Research Press, 1986.

Peck, M. Scott. *A Different Drum: Community Making and Peace.* New York: Simon and Schuster, 1987.

Peters, Thomas J. *Thriving on Chaos.* New York: Alfred A. Knopf, 1987.

Porter, Michael E. *Competitive Advantage: Creating and Sustaining Superior Performance.* New York: Free Press, 1985.

Reich, Robert B. *The Next American Frontier.* New York: Times Books, 1983.

Ross, Phillip J. *Taguchi Techniques for Quality Engineering.* New York: McGraw-Hill, 1988.

Ryan, John. "Consumers See Little Change in Product Quality." *Quality Progress,* December 1988.

―――. "1987 ASQC/Gallup Survey." *Quality Progress,* December 1987.

Ryan, Nancy E. "Tapping into Taguchi." *Manufacturing Engineering,* May 1987.

Schonberger, Richard J. *World Class Manufacturing: The Lessons of Simplicity Applied.* New York: Free Press, 1986.

Shingo, Shigeo. *A Revolution in Manufacturing: The SMED System.* Stamford, Conn.: Productivity, Inc., 1985.

―――. *Zero Quality Control: Source Inspection and the Poka-Yoke System.* Stamford, Conn.: Productivity, Inc., 1986.

―――. *Non-Stock Production.* Stamford, Conn.: Productivity, Inc. 1988.

Scholtes, Peter R. *The Team Handbook.* Madison, Wis.: Joiner Associates, 1988.

Sproul, R. C. *Stronger than Steel: The Wayne Alderson Story.* San Francisco: Harper & Row, 1980.

Sullivan, Lawrence P. "Quality Function Deployment." *Quality Progress,* June 1986, pp. 39–50.

―――. "The Power of Taguchi Methods." *Target,* Summer 1987.

Taguchi, Genichi. *Introduction to Quality Engineering.* Tokyo: Asian Productivity Organization, 1986.

INDEX